Y0-AGR-232

KETOGENIC MEDITERRANEAN DIET COOKBOOK

Ketogenic
Mediterranean Diet
Cookbook

Low Carb Mediterranean Recipes to Lose Weight Fast and
Feel Years Younger

Taylor Cora

LEGAL NOTICE

Copyright (c) 2018 by Taylor Cora

All rights are reserved. No portion of this book may be reproduced or duplicated using any form whether mechanical, electronic, or otherwise. No portion of this book may be transmitted, stored in a retrieval database, or otherwise made available in any manner whether public or private unless specific permission is granted by the publisher. Vector illustration credit: vec-teezy.com

This book does not offer advice, but merely provides information. The author offers no advice whether medical, financial, legal, or otherwise, nor does the author encourage any person to pursue any specific course of action discussed in this book. This book is not a substitute for professional advice. The reader accepts complete and sole responsibility for the manner in which this book and its contents are used. The publisher and the author will not be held liable for any damages caused.

"The greatest wealth

is health"

CONTENTS

FORWARD: A FUN WAY TO LIVE AND EAT

There are so many diets out there all claiming to be "the one" that will transform your life. How do you know which one is right for you? This book provides you with information on not one, not two, but three diets. The ketogenic diet, which has been very popular in recent years, slashes carbs in favor of fat. The Mediterranean diet, one of the most ancient eating plans out there, embraces whole grains, seafood, olive oil, and red wine. The third diet is a combination of the two, creating a hybrid that enhances the benefits of both. It could be "the one" diet for you.

The first diet covered is the ketogenic diet, which is abbreviated as "keto." Its defining feature is the tiny amount of carbs you're allowed to eat. 60-75% of your daily calories must come from fat, which triggers the body's production of ketones. This process is known as "ketosis." It has health benefits such as increased energy, easier weight loss, and sharper cognitive functions. It is a very restrictive diet, which makes it difficult for a lot of people. You aren't allowed to eat any grains, certain vegetables, most fruit, or anything with processed and artificial ingredients. You are allowed to eat full-fat dairy, however, which a lot of diets don't allow.

The Mediterranean diet, in contrast to the keto diet's narrow scope, is always listed as one of the most user-friendly diets out there. You are allowed to eat whole grains, beans, legumes, dairy, and a wide variety of veggies and meat, especially seafood. The diet has been associated with lowered cholesterol, easier weight loss, and long-term practicality. There's also a strong emphasis on one's social and mental health. The Mediterranean philosophy about food is that it should be as flavorful and satisfying as it is healthy. Moderation is key, so you are allowed to drink red wine. Reducing stress and an active social life are also important to the diet.

What happens when you combine the ketogenic and Mediterranean diet? You end up with a more restrictive Mediterranean diet with the benefits of ketosis. Many people find the hybrid not only delicious, but easier than the regular keto diet. There's more emphasis on flavor and fun than counting calories. The best diets always factor in one's social life and physical activity, and that's what the ketogenic Mediterranean diet does. Tips for success include eating slowly, getting high-quality sleep, and spending time with your loved ones. This book breaks down all the diets' allowed foods, benefits, downsides, and anything else you might need to know before deciding on a change. I give it my most enthusiastic seal of approval.

Georgio Kontos — Chef and Nutritionist

MY KETO JOURNEY THROUGH THE MEDITERRANEAN

For many years, I attempted changing my eating and experimenting with diets. Most of them didn't work out, but when I tried the Mediterranean diet, I finally started loving healthy food. Flavor is just as important as nutrition with this diet, and I learned how to love the process of cooking and eating with family. Eliminating packaged and processed foods was a bit of a challenge at first, but now, I don't even enjoy them. Real, whole foods with spices are just tastier than artificial ones or ingredients packed with additives.

Though I loved the Mediterranean diet, there were still some health goals I couldn't seem to reach. I started looking into how I could adapt my existing diet, which is when I read about the ketogenic diet. Using ketosis, the body is able to burn fat instead of glucose, which is stored as fat in the body when there's too much. To trigger this process, 60-75% of your daily calories must come from the fats found in full-fat dairy, nuts, seeds, coconut oil, and so on. Since I wanted to keep Mediterranean-friendly foods in my diet, I researched how the two diets could be combined.

This book is the product of my research. Getting the body into ketosis means cutting out a lot of carb-heavy foods, including whole grains, which are eaten on the Mediterranean diet. This was challenging, although it did get me to eat a lot more vegetables. I also appreciated how holding to Mediterranean foods allowed me to avoid certain downsides of the ketogenic diet, like eating too much dairy and red meat. When I was tempted to obsess over my ketone levels, I remembered that stress is just as poisonous to the body as unhealthy food. The Mediterranean diet taught me to relax more, spend time with my friends and family, and love life. It was a perfect balance to the ketogenic diet's more intense requirements.

In this book, you'll find thorough descriptions of the ketogenic, Mediterranean, and keto/Med diets. You'll learn how they work, what you can eat, what you *can't* eat, and the pros and cons. Going on a new diet can be overwhelming, and the best thing you can do before making a big change is to get informed. I hope this book guides you into making the best decision for your healthy living goals!

With Love,
Taylor Cora

INTRODUCTION

If you're reading this, you are probably looking to make a change. Maybe you have struggled to lose weight for a long time or you're worried about the impacts of artificial ingredients in today's packaged foods. Whatever the specific reason, this book can help. It provides a guide on the what and how of two famous diets -the ketogenic and Mediterranean diet - and the hybrid that uses the keto diet's food list and emphasizes Mediterranean ingredients and its philosophy. Food is fuel and most of us aren't fueling our bodies properly. By harnessing the process of ketosis, you can burn more fat, improve your energy levels, strengthen your resistant to disease, and more. Adding aspects of the Mediterranean diet like more olive oil and seafood helps fix some of the ketogenic diet's problems, while healthy habits like quality sleep and exercise enhance the benefits.

I. WHAT IS THE KETOGENIC DIET?

If you've heard of the ketogenic diet, you most likely believe it is simply a low-carb, high-fat diet. This is true, but there's more to the story. The keto diet is actually designed to mimic the effects of fasting, which has been prescribed to improve epilepsy for hundreds of years. In ancient Greece and Persia, doctors noticed that patients stopped having seizures when they stopped eating, so that became the standard treatment. It wasn't until the 20th-century that scientists figured out how to get the same results while allowing patients to eat. Consuming fewer calories and forgoing meat reduced seizures, and in 1921, an endocrinologist discovered that a low-carb, high-fat diet was also effective.

What is happening in the body when it fasts or eats lots of fat and few carbs? The liver produces three water soluble compounds known as ketones. These are what reduce seizures and gave the ketogenic diet its name. Dr. Russell Wilder from the Mayo Clinic coined the term in 1923 and developed the keto diet. It became very popular among epileptics, but fell out of use until the 1990's. Today, the low-carb aspect of the diet has been adopted by other eating plans like Atkin's. What is often missing from these copycats, however, is the high percentage of fat, which is what drives the diet's benefits.

Why is fat so important?

Most people eat a lot of carbs, which are necessary for energy and health. However, most of us also eat too many, and the excess glucose (what carbs turn into) is stored as body fat. On the keto diet, you're cutting down significantly on carbs. The body still needs fuel, though, which is why you have to fill in that gap with fat. While the body turns fat into a usable form of energy, the liver produces ketones. Your brain, muscles, and mitochondria all use ketones, and any that aren't used end up eliminated as waste. This process is known as "ketosis." To trigger ketosis, your daily calories must consist of at least 60-75% fat, with 15-30% from protein and only 5-10% from carbs. For most, that equals about 20 *net* carbs per day. You get net carbs by subtracting fiber from your total carbs.

The goal of the ketogenic diet is cut out enough carbs and eat enough fat to trigger ketosis, which is when the liver produces ketones and the body depends on fat instead of carbs for fuel.

How do you know when you're in ketosis?

If you're following the percentage breakdown of the keto diet, you should be firmly in ketosis within a few weeks. To know for sure, you can actually measure your ketone levels using urine strips, blood tests, or a breathalyzer. Urine strips measure for the acetoacetate ketone, while blood tests test for beta-hydroxybutyrate. Breathalyzers measure acetone. If your results are between 1.5-3.0 mmol/L (which stands for milligrams per decilitre), you're officially in ketosis and will be seeing the effects. Anything higher than 3.0 mmol/L won't give you superpowered health benefits, so don't try to raise your ketone levels beyond that. If you're diabetic, you actually want to stay below 1.6 mmol/L. This is because ketones turn the blood more acidic, making you vulnerable to ketoacidosis. For diabetics, this can be fatal if untreated.

The longer you're in ketosis, the fewer ketones your body eliminates, so your results with a blood, urine, or breath test will be lower. At this point, you'll be experiencing benefits, so frequent testing becomes unnecessary.

What you can and can't eat on the ketogenic diet

To get into (and stay) in ketosis, what do you have to eat? Lots of fat is clearly the priority, but you can't live on fat alone. Go through the lists below to find out what specific fats, proteins, vegetables, fruit, dairy, and so on you are allowed to eat while on the keto diet.

Fats

Since fat is the most important nutrient on the ketogenic diet, let's list the best sources. These oils, vegetable and animal fats, nuts, and dairy products will be excluded from their other categories for simplicity's sake.

- Coconut oil
- Coconut cream
- Cocoa butter
- Coconut butter
- Unsweetened coconut milk
- Full-fat Greek yogurt
- Olive oil
- Avocado oil
- Almond oil
- Full-fat grass-fed butter
- Ghee

- Duck fat
- Avocado
- All-natural unsweetened macadamia nut butter
- Macadamia nuts
- Brazil nuts
- Pecans
- Hemp seeds
- Wild-caught salmon
- Canned (in oil) sardines

Protein

On the ketogenic diet, 15-30% of your calories come from protein. The best sources come from meat, which should all be high-quality, grass-fed, pasture-raised, and so on.

- Grass-fed beef
- Pasture-raised, organic pork
- Free-range poultry
- Organic free-range eggs
- Organ meats
- Wild game
- Wild-caught seafood

Vegetables

Most vegetables are allowed on the ketogenic diet because they contain so many nutrients and fiber. There are some that are best eaten in moderation because their carb-to-fiber ratio is too low. If it's a starchy root vegetable, odds are you should avoid it. Note that fresh or frozen vegetables contain the same nutritional profile.

- Dark leafy greens
- Garlic
- Onion
- Cauliflower
- Cucumber
- Celery
- Broccoli
- Zucchini
- Bell peppers
- Radishes
- Cabbage
- Sea vegetables
- Fermented vegetables

Full-fat dairy

Dairy is a great source of both fat and protein, but it isn't meant to comprise the main part of your meal. It's easy to go crazy on the cheese, so use it as a snack or as a way to compliment other parts of a dish. Remember, whatever you get on this list should be full-fat. The only dairy *not* allowed on the keto diet is cow's milk because it's full of sugar.

- Cottage cheese
- Cream cheese
- Greek yogurt
- Cheddar cheese
- Mozzarella cheese
- Parmesan cheese
- Swiss cheese
- Ricotta cheese
- Mascarpone cheese
- Brie cheese
- Bleu cheese
- Heavy whipping cream
- Unsweetened carrageenan-free almond milk
- Unsweetened macadamia nut milk

On the keto diet, you eat fat-rich oils; full-fat dairy; animal protein; low-carb veggies and fruit; nuts and seeds; grain-free baking supplies, and natural 0-calorie sweeteners. You cannot eat grains; packaged

foods; sugars; high-carb vegetables and fruit; beans and legumes; and anything that's "low-fat" or "non-fat."

Fruit

The list of keto-friendly fruit is relatively short, because most fruit contains too much sugar. Even the ones you can eat on the diet, like berries, should be eaten in moderation. There are a few on this list listed as "higher on the GI scale," which means you should eat those very rarely. Take note that since tomato is technically a fruit, we include it here instead of in the vegetable section.

- Tomatoes
- Raspberries
- Strawberries
- Blackberries
- Cranberries
- Lemons

- Limes
- Plums
- Coconut
- Blueberries (higher on the GI scale)
- Peaches (higher on the GI scale)
- Oranges (higher on the GI scale)

Nuts + seeds

Nuts and seeds are perfect ketogenic snacks as they provide a burst of fat and protein. The keyword here is "snack," since more than a small handful can tip you out of ketosis. The best nuts and seeds were already listed in the "Fat" section, but the ones below are also good choices; they're just not *the best*.

- Almonds
- Sunflower seeds
- Pumpkin seeds

- Chia seeds
- Flaxseeds

Drinks

While water is the most obviously keto-friendly beverage, there are a few others you can have to break up the monotony. Whatever you drink should be unsweetened (0-calorie artificial sweeteners are out, too) and all-natural.

- Water
- Unsweetened coffee
- Unsweetened black tea

- Unsweetened herbal tea
- Sparkling water + seltzers
- Unsweetened coconut water

Other

What about cooking and baking supplies? Regular grain flours aren't allowed, but there are grain-free alternatives and natural 0-calorie sweeteners you can buy:

- Herbs + spices

- Almond flour

- Coconut flour
- Almond meal
- Flax meal
- Stevia/erythritol blends
- Monk fruit sweetener blends
- Sukrin Gold brown sugar substitute/Ideal Brown substitute
- Natural dark cocoa powder
- Rodelle pure vanilla extract (no-sugar added)
- Bakto fruit extracts
- Bakto nut extracts
- Baking powder
- Baking soda
- Psyllium husk
- Xanthan gum

What you <u>can't</u> eat on the ketogenic diet

For a quick rundown of what you *aren't* allowed to eat on this low-carb, high-fat diet, check out the list below. Anything that's high in carbs and low in fiber is high on the GI scale, which stands for "glycemic index." High GI foods spike your blood sugar, which you don't want to happen. Here are the high GI foods you can't eat:

- All grains (i.e. wheat, quinoa, buckwheat, rye, rice)
- High GI vegetables (i.e. corn, root vegetables)
- High GI fruits (i.e. bananas, apples, mangos, grapes)
- Beans and legumes
- Processed meats
- Processed and packaged food
- Sugary treats
- Low-fat dairy products
- Most alcohol
- Store-bought condiments
- Inflammatory oils
- Natural high GI sweeteners (i.e. sugar, maple syrup, date sugar, agave)
- Artificial sweeteners

What are the benefits of the keto diet?

The ketogenic diet is considered a "restrictive" eating plan because it cuts out an entire food group - grains. Restrictive diets can be very challenging, but the keto diet comes with some pretty compelling benefits. Here are the five most-cited reasons to make the change:

Weight loss can be easier

On the ketogenic diet, you cut out a lot of foods that cause excess weight gain, such as refined carbs and processed foods. As we mentioned before, any glucose your body doesn't use gets stored as body fat, and most of us don't need the large amount of carbs we eat. When you cut down on carbs and replace them with fat, it's much easier to lose weight. As for the carbs you *do* eat, these are the slower-burning ones that keep you feeling full for long periods of time. You are much less likely to snack between meals, which is a huge driver for extra pounds.

Your mind becomes sharper

One of the things people notice after being on the keto diet is that their minds are much clearer and they're able to focus for longer periods of time. This is most likely because your brain loves ketones, so eating lots of brain-healthy foods like avocados and eggs makes a big difference in your cognitive functions. There's also evidence that suggests ketones can help protect your mind from neurological conditions like Parkinson's and Alzheimer's.

You have more energy

When you cut out refined carbs and packaged foods packed with sugar, you'll suddenly become more energized. Eating GI foods causes your blood sugar levels to spike and then crash, resulting in mid-morning and afternoon slumps. When you're following the keto diet, your blood sugar levels are evened out and you have a steady supply of energy (from fat) that lasts through your whole day.

You sleep better

Everyone needs sleep, but not everyone gets the quality they need. Research has shown that keto dieters spend more time in REM sleep than those on a regular high-carb diet. That REM sleep is the sleep that restores you, allowing you to start each day well-rested. Good sleep is the foundation of good health, so it's definitely worth noting that the ketogenic diet can help you in that area.

You'll be protected against chronic inflammation

Chronic inflammation is a major problem. It leads to a host of diseases like arthritis, inflammatory bowel disease, Crohn's, asthma, hepatitis, and even cancer. Research suggests that high GI foods are part of the issue, so cutting those out can help protect you and even treat existing conditions. Lots of keto-friendly foods actively reduce inflammation as well, such as dark leafy greens, fatty fish, berries, and so on.

Benefits of ketosis include easier weight loss, better cognitive focus, more energy, better sleep, and reduced chronic inflammation. As for the downsides, many people suffer during the transition, they find the diet too restrictive, they suffer from micronutrient deficiency, and they're more vulnerable to ketoacidosis.

What about downsides?

You know why the ketogenic diet is so popular these days, but what are the problems? Knowing why some people end up not choosing the diet or stop it helps you better anticipate challenges and make an informed decision about your own health. There are four issues that experts point out:

The transition is hard

All the benefits we listed above start happening once you're in ketosis, but while you're getting there, it can be a really difficult transition. A lot of people experience the "keto flu," which is essentially withdrawal from carbs. The more carbs you're used to, the worse the withdrawal is. Symptoms include nausea, headaches, and irritability. It can be hard to predict how bad you'll feel or how long the transition will take. Many people don't want to put themselves through such an unpleasant experience. One solution is to transition slowly by gradually cutting out carbs. You'll just have to wait longer to enter ketosis and start seeing benefits.

It's too restrictive to be practical for the long-term

There are a lot of foods you can't eat on the ketogenic diet, and it can be difficult to avoid those ingredients. A lot of people follow the diet for a short period of time as a way to "reset" their health, but for the long-term, going keto can be really hard. An eating lifestyle that's so restrictive can be emotionally-taxing and lead to cheating, which can throw you out of ketosis. What's the point if that happens? It can be tempting to go back to unhealthy eating habits because the keto diet is so demanding.

Too many ketones have negative consequences

You can have too much of a good thing on the ketogenic diet. A high number of ketones actually makes your blood more acidic, which causes a condition known as ketoacidosis. For diabetics, this can be fatal if untreated. Symptoms include stomach pains, nausea, vomiting, and dehydration. Acidic blood damages your kidneys and liver if you don't do anything about it. That's why that range of 1.5 - 3 mmol/L (and just 1.5 mmol/L for diabetics) is important to maintain.

It eliminates too many nutrients

Nutritionists aren't very fond of the keto diet because of the foods it eliminates. There are lots of important vitamins and minerals you don't get from their best sources, and it can lead to what's known as micronutrient deficiency. If you aren't careful to fill in those gaps with other foods or supplements, you can miss out on sodium, magnesium, and potassium. Not getting enough of these nutrients will result in dehydration, headaches, nausea, low energy, weak bones, and so on.

II. What is the Mediterranean diet?

The Mediterranean is famous for its food, which includes groves of olives, grape vineyards, sun-ripened tomatoes, and an abundance of fresh seafood. It wasn't until 1970, however, that Dr. Ancel and Margaret Keys (a biologist and chemist respectively) published studies on the health impacts. While working at the School of Public Health in Minnesota, Dr. Keys conducted a study of over 12,000 men from Finland, Holland, Japan Greece, Italy, Yugoslavia, and the United States.

This is now known as "The Seven Countries" study. It revealed that countries with high saturated fat and cholesterol intake experienced more cardiovascular disease and death. The US and Finland had the highest while Japan, Greece, and Italy had the lowest.

So, people knew since the 1970's that people in the Mediterranean were very healthy because of what they ate. It wasn't until 1993, however, that the name "Mediterranean Diet" was coined and described as a "delicious, pleasurable, and very healthful way to eat." The diet includes a lot of variety - vegetables, fruit, grains, legumes, fish, seafood, eggs, olive oil, and, of course, red wine.

A diet about more than food

Why does this diet work exactly? You are encouraged to eat real, whole foods free from refined sugars and other artificial ingredients. Fast food and packaged meals are not a part of the diet, which significantly lowers your intake of saturated fats. Instead, vegetables take up a lot of every plate and while you are allowed to eat red meat, heart-healthy fish and seafood make up the bulk of your animal protein. The variety of food also plays a huge role in its popularity because people are more likely to stick to an eating plan if meals are always interesting.

The reason the Mediterranean diet is so healthy doesn't break down to just simple nutritional consumption. The culture itself plays a huge role. Sharing meals with family and friends is hugely important, which means the ingredient of "love" has a real, tangible impact on people's health.

The Mediterranean lifestyle is also traditionally rich in outdoor activities like walking, farming, swimming, and so on. Your stress levels drop when you live like a Mediterranean, allowing the food you eat to heal and restore your body *and* mind. How you spend your time and your mental state are just as important as what you eat when you go on the Mediterranean diet.

The Mediterranean diet is all about fresh, whole foods like seafood and vegetables, and healthy fats like olive oil and olives. The only foods you eliminate are packaged and artificial; you are allowed to eat grain.

What you can and can't eat on the Mediterranean diet

Now you know the Mediterranean diet is very popular among nutritionists and eaters alike, but what exactly can you eat? There are no food groups eliminated (unless you consider "processed" a food group), and it's all about moderation and making good choices. Here are the proteins, fats, oils, vegetables, fruits, grains, and more that you'll be eating:

Protein

Most of your protein will come from seafood and lean poultry. Since Italy and Greece are right by the ocean, it's a culture rich in food right from the sea. You'll be eating a lot more fish than usual and less red meat. In fact, for maximum health benefits, you should be eating grass-fed steaks and other red meat only about once a month.

- Seafood (salmon, tuna, sardines, rainbow trout, shrimp)
- Poultry (skinless, boneless chicken + turkey breasts)
- Grass-fed red meat (infrequently i.e. once a month)
- Grass-fed pork (infrequently)
- Organic eggs

Oils + vinegars

Extra-virgin olive oil is one of the superstars of the Mediterranean diet. You use it in place of butter, vegetable oil, and other fats. Vinegar is also used a lot for flavor, so expect to see recipes that use balsamic vinegar and red wine vinegar, especially.

- EVOO
- Balsamic vinegar
- Red wine vinegar
- Apple cider vinegar

Vegetables

You can eat all the vegetables on this diet. Olives are especially popular because they grow so well on the Mediterranean islands and they're fatty. As usual, dark leafy greens are the most nutritionally-dense vegetables, while you should eat starchy, less nutritious veggies like potatoes in smaller amounts.

- Olives
- Onions
- Garlic
- Potatoes
- Artichokes
- Squash
- Eggplant
- Zucchini
- Carrots
- Beets
- Celery
- Dark leafy greens
- Bell peppers
- Cabbage
- Mushrooms
- Leeks
- Scallions
- Corn

- Cucumbers
- Broccoli

- Cauliflower

Whole grains

You can eat bread and pasta on this diet! If it's a whole-grain, it's a-okay on this diet. Here are the most commonly-used ones:

- Whole wheat
- Rice (brown and wild rice)
- Millet
- Buckwheat
- Quinoa

- Pasta
- Barley
- Bulgar
- Orzo

Beans + legumes

Beans and legumes are packed with protein and other important nutrients that help make the Mediterranean diet such a good choice. There are more than what this list includes, but you'll see these most frequently:

- Black beans
- Chickpeas
- Kidney beans
- Green beans

- Black-eyed peas
- Lentils
- Split peas

Dairy

Greek yogurt is obviously on this list, as is feta, mozzarella, ricotta, and parmesan. You're also allowed to eat cheddar and other types of cheese, but you'll see a lot more of the feta, mozz, ricotta, and parm, which are naturally lower in saturated fats. You can also eat butter, but most of the time it's replaced by olive oil. Cow's milk is also something you can use/drink, but very rarely.

- Greek yogurt
- Cottage cheese
- Cream cheese
- Cheddar cheese
- Feta cheese
- Ricotta cheese
- Mozzarella cheese
- Parmesan cheese

- Swiss cheese
- Mascarpone cheese
- Brie cheese
- Bleu cheese
- Butter
- Heavy whipping cream
- Unsweetened nut milks
- Cow's milk

Fruit

You aren't limited when it comes to fruit options on the Mediterranean diet; you just want to be smart about how much you eat. In this diet, moderation is everything.

You'll see a lot of tomatoes in recipes as well as berries and figs for desserts.

- Tomatoes
- Avocado
- Citrus (lemons, oranges, limes)
- Grapes
- Peaches
- Nectarines
- Watermelon

- Apricots
- Apples
- Pears
- Berries (strawberries, blackberries, etc)
- Figs
- Kiwi

Nuts + seeds

Nuts and seeds are a valuable source of fat and protein. They're the perfect palm-sized snack and they're best in that small amount. They can also be used to dress salads, add crunch to granolas, and more.

- Walnuts
- Almonds
- Pine nuts
- Sesame seeds

- Sunflower seeds
- Pumpkin seeds
- Flax seeds
- Chia seeds

Drinks

You can drink a pretty wide assortment of beverages, including coffee, tea, and fresh juice. Red wine is also a really big part of Mediterranean culture, but keep in mind it won't improve your health if you aren't healthy. If you're eating well, you can have a daily serving (4-ounce max for women, 8-ounces max for men) of red wine per day. As for milk, you can't drink a lot, stock up on your favorite unsweetened nut milk.

- Water
- Coffee
- Tea

- Red wine
- Fresh juice
- Unsweetened nut milks

Sweeteners

You don't eliminate any sweeteners on the Mediterranean diet, but it's highly-recommended that you use them infrequently.

Honey is the most commonly-used sweetener on this diet, but you consume it in very small amounts. If you have a sweet tooth, consider using a natural 0-calorie sweetener like stevia.

- Honey (in small amounts)
- Maple syrup (in small amounts)
- Dates

- Raisins
- Stevia/erythritol blends

Other

What else should you always have in your pantry? A wide assortment of herbs and spices is always necessarily, especially those found in Greek and Italian food. You'll also have standard baking supplies like flour, baking powder, vanilla extract, and so on.

- Herbs and spices
- Whole-grain or whole-wheat flour
- Baking soda
- Baking powder
- All-natural flavor extracts
- Dark cocoa powder

Because there aren't a lot of "forbidden" foods on the Mediterranean diet, good choices and moderation are key.

What you can't eat on the Mediterranean diet

In order to enjoy the most benefits from this diet, there are certain foods you want to avoid or exclude completely. As you read the list, all the foods will make sense since pretty much every diet out there says not to eat them. That being said, you can treat yourself if something is high-quality. There's a big difference between a Snickers bar and a piece of dark Belgian chocolate.

- _Sugary treats_
- _Soft drinks_
- _Refined grains (white bread, white rice, cereal, bagels, etc)_
- _Processed packaged foods_
- _Processed meats (hot dogs, bacon, etc)_
- _Trans fats_
- _Refined oils (vegetable oil, soybean oil, etc)_
- _Artificial sweeteners_

What are the benefits of the Mediterranean diet?

There are so many reasons to switch to a Mediterranean diet, but what are they specifically? Here are the most cited benefits:

It lowers cholesterol

When people talk about the Mediterranean diet, they talk about how good it is for your heart. The first major study - the Seven Countries study - connected the dots between living in a Mediterranean country and having less cardiovascular disease. Other studies have shown that the diet effectively lowers cholesterol and triglycerides in a lot of people. When combined with exercise, you have a good recipe for a healthy heart. It is worth noting that a much-cited study from 2013 (which said people on Mediterranean diet were less likely to experience cardiac events) was retracted. The correction simply "softened" the language, however, so it isn't as if the conclusions were reversed.

It reduces the risk of certain conditions

Heart disease isn't the only problem the Mediterranean diet can help with. One study showed that sticking to the diet can lower your risk of dementia by up to ⅓. The healthy fats found in olive oil, fatty fish, and avocado protect you against other brain conditions, too. Even your risk of cancer is affected by the Mediterranean diet, with one study showing that following the diet very closely can reduce your risk of dying from a cancer.

It can make weight loss easier

If one of your health goals is to lose weight, the Mediterranean diet can help. When you cut out processed food and refined sugar, you're eliminating the driving force behind weight gain. Eating lots of fiber-rich vegetables like darky leafy greens can also fill you up faster, so you eat loss overall. At least one paper specifically showed that people eating lots of nuts and olive oil lost more weight than those on a low-fat diet.

> **The Mediterranean diet's benefits include lowered cholesterol, protection against certain disease and easier weight loss. It's also a very doable diet for the long-term.**

It's the perfect long-term diet

One of the best things about the Mediterranean diet is that it's one of the easiest diets to follow. That means you can stick to it for a long time without drastically changing your life or restricting what you eat. A lot of variety and flavor is strongly-emphasized, so you never feel like you're eating "diet" food. The diet can also be easily customized for your specific health needs and goals, like adapting it to be ketogenic.

Are there any downsides?

The Mediterranean diet doesn't have a lot wrong with it, but there are just a few possible cons you should know about, so you can be as informed as possible before diving in. There are three issues:

You may not get enough calcium

While you are allowed to eat dairy, you don't eat a lot. You mostly eat it in the form of low-fat cheeses, but even then, you might not get enough calcium. The solution is simple: eat vegetable sources like collards, mustard greens, and kale. You can also drink almond milk that's been fortified with calcium.

It's easy to go overboard on the not-as healthy foods

The downside to a diet that's so varied is eating too much of one specific thing or just eating too much. For a lot of people, red wine is their vice. Remember, you want to drink just 1-2 glasses per day. You also still need to limit your consumption of food in general in order to meet health goals. Moderation is key, but when the food tastes so good, it can be easy to overeat.

You have to cook a lot

The Mediterranean diet does not allow very much eating out. You also can't buy prepared, packaged meals, so that means you cook all your meals and snacks. There are lots of recipes designed to be simple and quick, but if you aren't used to cooking very much, there's still an adjustment. It's definitely worth it, however.

III. COMBINING THE KETOGENIC AND MEDITERRANEAN DIETS

Now that you know what the ketogenic and Mediterranean diets are, why should you think about combining them? First, they offer similar health benefits, making them compatible. Both lower cholesterol and focus on the nutrients found in fresh vegetables. They also both eliminate artificial foods, refined sugar, and additives. The main reason to hybridize them, however, is that the Mediterranean diet can make the ketogenic diet healthier.

How does the Mediterranean diet improve the keto diet?

The ketogenic diet is often criticized because it can lead to micronutrient deficiency. It can also become an unbalanced diet too full of red meat, dairy, and not enough vegetables. When you emphasise Mediterranean foods like olive oil and seafood, it can help restore balance and nutrients to your eating. To fill in the space left by reducing red meat and dairy, you can easily add more vegetables. More health benefits result.

The philosophy of the Mediterranean diet also impacts the ketogenic diet in a very positive way. When you're trying to get (and stay) in ketosis, you will be tempted to focus too much on numbers - the number of carbs you're eating, your ketone level, how many calories you're eating, and so on. The Mediterranean diet emphasizes enjoying the food you make, cooking and eating with loved ones, and being active. This will prevent you from obsessing over every single thing you put on your plate and reduce your stress levels. Less stress has just as significant an impact on your health as what you eat, so you'll sleep better, have more energy, and an overall better life. The health benefits of both the Mediterranean and ketogenic diets will also manifest more powerfully in a body with less stress.

> **Combining the ketogenic and Mediterranean diet can make the restrictiveness of the keto diet a bit easier and healthier, since you focus a lot on seafood, vegetables, olive oil, and non-diet habits like exercise and spending time with loved ones.**

What you can and can't eat on the ketogenic Mediterranean diet

In terms of what you can eat on a keto/Mediterranean diet, you'll be following the keto list while emphasizing certain foods that overlap with the Mediterranean. Those foods are bolded in the sections below. The grain, beans, and legume sections are eliminated.

Fats

To get into ketosis, you need to eat a lot of fat, specifically, 60-75% of your daily calories. For the Mediterranean aspect, focus on olive oil as your primary cooking fat over coconut oil, butter, and so on. Other good fats for this combo diet include Greek yogurt, avocados, olives, and fish.

- Coconut oil
- Coconut cream
- Cocoa butter
- Coconut butter
- Unsweetened coconut milk
- **Full-fat Greek yogurt**
- **Olive oil**
- Avocado oil
- Almond oil
- Full-fat grass-fed butter
- Ghee

- Duck fat
- **Avocado**
- **Olives**
- All-natural unsweetened macadamia nut butter
- Macadamia nuts
- Brazil nuts
- Pecans
- Hemp seeds
- **Wild-caught salmon**
- **Canned (in oil) sardines**

Protein

When you combine the ketogenic and Mediterranean diets, you want to significantly limit how much beef you eat. Strongly emphasize seafood instead, followed by eggs and chicken.

- Grass-fed beef
- Pasture-raised, organic pork
- **Free-range poultry**
- **Organic free-range eggs**

- Organ meats
- Wild game
- **Wild-caught seafood**

Vegetables

The emphasized vegetables are the ones you'll see most in Mediterranean-inspired recipes. All the vegetables listed are keto-friendly; starchy, root veggies are eliminated.

- Dark leafy greens
- Garlic
- Onion
- Cauliflower
- Cucumber
- Celery
- Broccoli

- Zucchini
- Tomatoes
- Bell peppers
- Radishes
- Cabbage
- Sea vegetables
- Fermented vegetables

Full-fat dairy

You don't eat as much dairy on the ketogenic Mediterranean diet as you would on the basic keto diet. Your sources will mostly come from low-fat cheeses like mozzarella, parmesan, feta, and ricotta. Depend on other sources for the fat you need to maintain ketosis; dairy is mostly just a way to add a bit of variety and flavor into your meals and snacks.

- Cottage cheese

- Cream cheese

- Cheddar cheese
- **Mozzarella cheese**
- **Parmesan cheese**
- Swiss cheese
- **Feta cheese**
- **Ricotta cheese**
- Mascarpone cheese

- Brie cheese
- Bleu cheese
- Heavy whipping cream
- **Unsweetened carrageenan-free almond milk**
- Unsweetened macadamia nut milk

Fruit

You will pretty much eat the same fruits you would on the basic keto diet, because they're still full of carbs and can kick you out of ketosis. You'll be eating berries and some citrus fruits.

- Berries (strawberries, raspberries, cranberries, etc)
- Lemons
- Limes
- Plums

- Coconut
- Blueberries (higher on the GI scale)
- Peaches (higher on the GI scale)
- Oranges (higher on the GI scale)

On the ketogenic Mediterranean diet, you follow the keto diet's food list, but emphasize the Mediterranean foods like seafood, olive oil, and certain cheeses.

Nuts + seeds

Nuts and seeds are still a great snack and quick source of protein and fat. Remember to eat only a handful at a time or so.

- Almonds
- Sunflower seeds
- Pumpkin seeds

- Chia seeds
- Flaxseeds

Drinks

The biggest question in this section is the wine question. Yes, you can drink red wine and enter ketosis. You just have to be choosy and drink less frequently than if you were following the traditional Mediterranean diet. Your other beverage options include sparkling waters with natural ingredients, unsweetened coconut water, black coffee, and so on.

- Water
- Unsweetened coffee
- Unsweetened black tea
- Unsweetened herbal tea

- Sparkling water + seltzers
- Unsweetened coconut water
- **Red wine**

Other

For baking and cooking supplies, everything needs to be grain-free and all-natural. This list is identical to the one found in the ketogenic diet section, with some vinegars added from the Mediterranean diet at the end. All sweeteners should be natural and 0-calorie.

- Herbs + spices
- Almond flour
- Coconut flour
- Almond meal
- Flax meal
- Stevia/erythritol blends
- Monk fruit sweetener blends
- Sukrin Gold brown sugar substitute/Ideal Brown substitute
- Natural dark cocoa powder
- Rodelle pure vanilla extract (no-sugar added)
- Bakto fruit extracts
- Bakto nut extracts
- Baking powder
- Baking soda
- Psyllium husk
- Xanthan gum
- Balsamic vinegar
- Apple cider vinegar
- Red wine vinegar

Tips for success

The ketogenic diet is difficult and the Mediterranean diet is considered easier. When you combine them, you get a diet that's relatively strict because of the ketogenic aspects. You can't eat grains, beans, or other high-carb foods, and you have to eat a certain percentage of fat to enter ketosis. However, there are tips you can implement from the Mediterranean lifestyle and through smart planning that help make the keto diet better for the long-term.

Prep your meals

You'll be cooking a lot on the keto Mediterranean diet. The meals don't have to be complicated, but you do have to be somewhat organized in order to get the right percentages of fat, protein, and carbs necessary to stay in ketosis. The easiest way to do this is to prep your meals. This means planning what you're going to eat a week or so in advance, writing grocery lists, and doing any prep or cooking you can for all your meals on a designated day. People often choose Sunday. Doing this ultimately saves you lots of time during the week when you're busier and ensures each meal has all the nutrition you need.

Get active

Exercise is important for both ketosis and adhering to the Mediterranean philosophy. Physical activity actually helps the body get into ketosis and stay there. Certain workouts are better than others. Endurance training and core/flexibility workouts naturally use fat as fuel instead of carbs, so you'll be sure to have the energy you need. These are also great workouts to engage in with friends and family because you can chat at the same time.

Sleep well

High-quality sleep is extremely-restorative and necessary for good health. If you want to enjoy all the benefits from the keto Mediterranean diet, be sure to practice good sleep hygiene. This includes getting an uninterrupted 8 hours per night, not having electronics in your bedroom, and making sure the room is completely dark. You might experience some initial insomnia when you're beginning to enter ketosis, but studies have shown that ketosis can actually result in more REM sleep.

To succeed on the restrictive ketogenic Mediterranean diet, practice good habits like prepping your meals, staying active, adopting good sleep hygiene, drinking enough water, eating slowly, and reducing your stress by spending time with friends and family.

Stay hydrated

Most people don't drink enough water. Hydration is especially important when you're beginning to enter ketosis because you lose more liquid than usual. Always have water or another keto-friendly beverage on hand, like unsweetened coconut water. For something hot and nutritious, try bone broth.

Eat slowly and savor your food

One of the easiest things you can do to help your health is slow down when you're eating. Slow eating has a lot of benefits including better digestion, better hydration, and less overeating. It also fits perfectly with the Mediterranean philosophy of really enjoying your food and savoring the flavors. You'll be cooking a lot and trying a variety of recipes on this diet; you deserve the chance to really taste what you've made.

Make time for loved ones

The last (but certainly not the least important) tip for success is to make time for your friends and family. Humans are built for community, but unfortunately, our hectic society has forgotten that. It is easy to get pulled into work and stress out about our own problems without seeking love and connection with the people around us. Spending time with those you love is medicine for the soul and body. It reduces your stress and increases your happiness, which has a huge positive impact on every area of your life.

RED MEAT

Contents

Sautéed Beef Pepper with Cheese and Parsley Topping

Serves: 4 / Preparation time: 8 minutes / Cooking time: 22 minutes

1 lb. beef rib eye steak

2 tablespoons extra virgin olive oil

¼ cup chopped onion

½ teaspoon pepper

¼ cup goat cheese

2 teaspoons minced parsley

½ teaspoon grated garlic

½ teaspoon thyme

- Cut the beef rib eye steak into thin slices then set aside.
- Preheat a skillet over medium heat then pour olive oil into the skillet.
- Once the oil is hot, stir in chopped onion and sauté until aromatic.
- Next, add sliced beef to the skillet then season with pepper. Cook until done.
- Transfer the sautéed beef to a serving dish then set aside.
- Quickly combine goat cheese with minced parsley, grated garlic, and thyme then mix until incorporated and smooth.
- Serve the sautéed beef with the cheese mixture and enjoy immediately.

Per Serving: Net Carbs: 1g; Calories: 383; Total Fat: 32.5g; Saturated Fat: 11.3g
Protein: 20.9g; Carbs: 1.6g; Fiber: 0.6g; Sugar: 0.4g

Fat 76% / Protein 23% / Carbs 1%

Spicy Beef Tender with Healthy Cucumber

Serves: 4 / Preparation time: 9 minutes / Cooking time: 23 minutes

1 lb. beef rib eye

2 tablespoons extra virgin olive oil

2 teaspoons minced garlic

2 teaspoons sliced shallot

2 tablespoons red chili flakes

1-cup water

1 cup chopped cucumber

- Cut the beef rib eye into thin slices then set aside.
- Preheat a skillet over medium heat then pour extra virgin olive oil into it.
- Stir in minced garlic and sliced shallot to the skillet then sauté until lightly golden brown and aromatic.
- Add sliced beef to the skillet then stir until just wilted.
- After that, pour water over the beef then bring to boil.
- Once it is boiled, reduce the heat and cook until the water is completely absorbed into the beef and the beef is tender.
- Next, stir in red chili flakes and chopped cucumber to the skillet then sauté and cook until wilted.
- Once it is done, remove the cooked beef from the heat and transfer to a serving dish.
- Serve and enjoy.

Per Serving: Net Carbs: 3.2g; Calories: 386; Total Fat: 32.1g; Saturated Fat: 11g
Protein: 20.7g; Carbs: 3.7g; Fiber: 0.5g; Sugar: 1.6g

Fat 75% / Protein 22% / Carbs 3%

Zucchini Beef Casserole

Serves: 4 / Preparation time: 14 minutes / Cooking time: 38 minutes

½ cup goat cheese

2 tablespoons coconut yogurt

2 eggs

1-cup ground beef

2 tablespoons extra virgin olive oil

¼ cup chopped onion

1-cup water

½ teaspoon pepper

¼ teaspoon ginger

¼ teaspoon turmeric

¾ cup coconut flour

4 tablespoons coconut oil

½ cup sliced zucchini

- Preheat a skillet over medium heat then pour extra virgin olive oil into the skillet.
- Once the oil is hot, stir in chopped onion and sauté until lightly golden brown and aromatic.
- Add ground beef to the skillet then season with pepper, ginger, and turmeric. Stir until the beef is no longer pink.
- Pour water over the beef then bring to boil.
- Once it is boiled, reduce the heat and cook until the water is completely absorbed into the beef.
- Once it is done, remove the beef from heat and let it cool.
- Preheat an oven to 400°F (204°C) and coat a casserole dish with cooking spray. Set aside.
- Transfer the cooked beef to the prepared casserole dish then spread evenly.
- Combine goat cheese with eggs and coconut yogurt then stir until incorporated.
- Pour the cheese mixture over the beef and arrange sliced zucchini on it.
- Pour coconut oil over the coconut flour then mix until becoming crumbles.
- Sprinkle the crumbles on top then bake the casserole for approximately 35 minutes or until set.
- Once it is done, remove the casserole from the oven and let it cool.
- Serve and enjoy.

Per Serving: Net Carbs: 2.4g; Calories: 381; Total Fat: 35.2g; Saturated Fat: 17.3g
Protein: 13.3g; Carbs: 3.8g; Fiber: 1.4g; Sugar: 1.6 g

Fat 83% / Protein 14% / Carbs 3%

Beef Broccoli Crunchy Nugget

Serves: 4 / Preparation time: 12 minutes / Cooking time: 23 minutes

1 lb. ground beef

3 eggs

2 tablespoons coconut flour

½ teaspoon pepper

2 teaspoons minced garlic

2 cups chopped broccoli

1 cup grated coconut

- Preheat a steamer over medium heat and line a baking pan with aluminum foil. Set aside.
- Combine ground beef with 2 eggs, coconut flour, pepper, minced garlic, and chopped broccoli in a food processor then process until smooth.
- Transfer the mixture to the prepared baking pan then spread evenly.
- Place the baking pan in the steamer then steam the nugget for approximately 20 minutes or until set.
- Once it is done, remove the baking pan from the steamer and let it cool.
- When the nugget is already cool, take it out of the baking pan then cut into thick slices.
- Crack the remaining egg then place in a bowl. Stir the egg until just incorporated.
- Dip each nugget into the egg then roll in the grated coconut.
- Refrigerate the beef nugget for at least 2 hours.
- Once you want to serve it, remove the beef nugget from the refrigerator and fry.
- Serve and enjoy.

Per Serving: Net Carbs: 5.3g; Calories: 496; Total Fat: 39.1g; Saturated Fat: 18.9g
Protein: 25.2g; Carbs: 10.9g; Fiber: 5.6g; Sugar: 2.8g

Fat 71% / Protein 25% / Carbs 4%

Warm Oxtail Soup with Nutmeg and Cloves

Serves: 4 / Preparation time: 3 minutes / Cooking time: 44 minutes

1-¼ lbs. beef rib eye

2 tablespoons sliced shallots

¾ teaspoon nutmeg

3 cloves

¾ teaspoon pepper

5 cups water

½ cup sliced carrots

½ cup cauliflower florets

¼ cup chopped leek

2 tablespoons celeries

- Cut the beef into medium pieces then place in a pot.
- Pour water into a pot then bring t boil.
- Once it is boiled, reduce the heat and season the beef with sliced shallots, nutmeg, clove, and pepper. Cook for approximately 30 minutes or until the beef is tender.
- Next, add sliced carrots, leek, and cauliflower florets to the pot then stir well. Cook until the vegetables are wilted but not too soft.
- When the soup is done, remove from heat and transfer to a serving bowl.
- Sprinkle chopped celeries on top and serve warm.
- Enjoy immediately.

Per Serving: Net Carbs: 3.5g; Calories: 409; Total Fat: 31.6g; Saturated Fat: 12.6g
Protein: 25.7g; Carbs: 4.7g; Fiber: 1.2g; Sugar: 1.5g

Fat 70% / Protein 27% / Carbs 3%

Spiced Pork Shoulder with Goat Cheese and Tender Veggies

Serves: 4 / Preparation time: 9 minutes / Cooking time: 19 minutes

1 lb. pork shoulder

2 tablespoons extra virgin olive oil

¾ teaspoon pepper

1-½ teaspoons thyme

¼ teaspoon grated lemon zest

¼ cup goat cheese

2 tablespoons almond butter

1 cup chopped green beans

½ cup sliced carrots

¼ cup chicken broth

1 tablespoon lemon juice

- Combine goat cheese with almond butter, grated lemon zest, thyme, and ¼ teaspoon of pepper then mix until incorporated. Set aside.
- Preheat a pan over medium heat then pour extra virgin olive oil into it.
- Once the oil is hot, sprinkle the ¼ teaspoon of pepper over the pork then place them on the pan.
- Cook the pork for approximately 4 minutes then flip it.
- Continue cooking the pork until both sides are lightly golden brown and the pork is completely cooked.
- Once it is done, remove the cooked pork from the pan and place on a serving dish.
- Next, add green beans and carrots to the pan then pour chicken broth into the pan. Season the vegetables with the remaining pepper then bring to boil.
- Once it is boiled, reduce the heat and cook until the vegetables are tender.
- Remove the tender vegetables from the heat and drizzle lemon juice over the vegetables. Place the vegetables next to the cooked pork.
- Top the pork with goat cheese mixture then serve.
- Enjoy warm.

Per Serving: Net Carbs: 3.1g; Calories: 423; Total Fat: 35.1g; Saturated Fat: 9.7g
Protein: 22g; Carbs: 5.4g; Fiber: 2.3g; Sugar: 1.6g

Fat 75% / Protein 22% / Carbs 3%

Paprika and Cayenne Pulled Pork Butt with Roasted Asparagus

Serves: 4 / Preparation time: 2 hours / Cooking time: 2 hours 34 minutes

1 lb. pork butt

2 teaspoons cayenne pepper

2 teaspoons paprika

2-½ teaspoons pepper

2 tablespoons mustard

1 bunch asparagus spears

2-½ tablespoons extra virgin olive oil

½ teaspoon minced garlic

1 tablespoon lemon juice

- Rub the pork butt with cayenne pepper, paprika, pepper, and mustard then marinate for at least 2 hours or more. Store in the fridge to keep it fresh.
- After 2 hours, remove the pork butt from the fridge and thaw at room temperature.
- Preheat an oven to 350°F (177°C) and line a baking tray with aluminum foil.
- Once the oven is ready, place the marinated pork butt on the prepared baking tray and cover with aluminum foil.
- Bake the pork butt for approximately 2 hours or until tender then remove from the oven. Let it rest for a few minutes.
- In the meantime, cut and trim the asparagus then toss with extra virgin olive oil, minced garlic, and lemon juice.
- Line a baking tray with aluminum foil then spread the seasoned asparagus on it.
- Bake the asparagus for about 20 hours or until tender.
- Once it is done, remove the asparagus from the oven and let it rest.
- Slowly unwrap the pork butt then using a fork shred the cooked pork.
- Place the pulled pork on a serving dish then serve with roasted asparagus.
- Serve and enjoy.

Per Serving: Net Carbs: 2.6g; Calories: 353; Total Fat: 29g; Saturated Fat: 9.2g
Protein: 20.4g; Carbs: 4.9g; Fiber: 2.3g; Sugar: 1.1g

Fat 74% / Protein 23% / Carbs 3%

Stuffed Pork Black Pepper Jalapeno with Carrots

Serves: 4 / Preparation time: 14 minutes / Cooking time: 18 minutes

½ lb. green jalapenos

¾ lb. ground pork

½ cup goat cheese

2 tablespoons diced onion

2 tablespoons grated carrots

½ teaspoon black pepper

2 eggs

2 tablespoons extra virgin olive oil

- Cut the green jalapenos into halves lengthwise then remove the seeds. Set aside.
- Crack the eggs then place the eggs in a bowl.
- Pour extra virgin olive oil into the eggs then season with black pepper. Stir until incorporated.
- Combine ground pork with goat cheese, diced onion, and grated carrot in a bowl then pour the egg mixture over the pork. Mix well.
- Preheat a steamer over medium heat then wait until it is ready.
- Fill each halved jalapeno with the pork mixture then arrange in the steamer.
- Steam the filled jalapenos for approximately 20 minutes or until set.
- Once it is done, remove the stuffed jalapenos from the steamer and arrange on a serving dish.
- If you like, you can bake the steamed jalapenos until lightly golden brown.
- Serve and enjoy warm.

Per Serving: Net Carbs: 5.1g; Calories: 343; Total Fat: 27.2g; Saturated Fat: 8.2g
Protein: 17.8g; Carbs: 5.4g; Fiber: 0.3g; Sugar: 0.6g

Fat 71% / Protein 23% / Carbs 6%

Spicy Pork with Kale Garlic

Serves: 4 / Preparation time: 16 minutes / Cooking time: 19 minutes

1 lb. pork shoulder

¼ lb. pork rind

5 teaspoons minced garlic

2 shallots

¼ cup red chilies

2 lemon grasses

2 kaffir lime leaves

1 bay leaf

2 cups water

½ cup coconut milk

2 cups chopped kale

2 tablespoons extra virgin olive oil

- Place red chilies in a pan then pour water to cover. Bring to boil.
- Once it is boiled, reduce the heat and cook until the red chilies are wilted.
- Remove the red chilies from heat and strain the water.
- Transfer the red chilies to a food processor then add 3 teaspoons minced garlic and shallots then process until smooth. Set aside.
- Cut the pork shoulder and pork rind into cubes then place in a skillet.
- Add the spice mixture to the skillet then pour water over the pork.
- Season the pork with lemon grasses, kaffir lime leaves, and bay leaf then bring to boil.
- Once it is boiled, reduce the heat and cook the pork until tender. The gravy will be reduced into half.
- In the meantime, preheat another skillet and pour extra virgin olive oil into it.
- Stir in minced garlic to the skillet then sauté until aromatic and wilted.
- Next, add chopped kale to the skillet then sauté until wilted.
- Remove the sautéed kale from heat then set aside.
- When the pork is tender, pour coconut milk over the pork then bring to a simmer.
- Transfer the cooked pork to a serving dish then serve with sautéed kale.
- Enjoy warm.

Per Serving: Net Carbs: 7g; Calories: 454; Total Fat: 37.5g; Saturated Fat: 15.5g
Protein: 21.7g; Carbs: 8.3g; Fiber: 1.3g; Sugar: 1g

Fat 74% / Protein 20% / Carbs 6%

Pork Coconut Curry in Lettuce Blanket

Serves: 4 / Preparation time: 16 minutes / Cooking time: 21 minutes

¾ lb. boneless pork shoulder

2 tablespoons extra virgin olive oil

2 teaspoons minced garlic

2 teaspoons sliced shallot

1-teaspoon curry powder

½ teaspoon turmeric

1-teaspoon pepper

2 cups water

½ cup coconut milk

1 handful of fresh lettuce

- Cut the boneless pork shoulder into small dices then set aside.
- Preheat a skillet over medium heat then pour extra virgin olive oil into the skillet.
- Once t is hot, stir in minced garlic and sliced shallot to the skillet and sauté until wilted and aromatic.
- Add diced pork to the skillet then cook until the pork is just wilted.
- Season the pork with curry powder, turmeric, and pepper then pour water over the pork bring to boil.
- Once it is boiled, reduce the heat and cook until the pork is tender and the water is completely absorbed into the pork.
- Next, drizzle coconut milk over the pork and bring to a simmer.
- Occasionally stir the pork and cook until there is no more liquid in the skillet.
- Remove the pork from heat and let it cool.
- Take a large lettuce and place on a flat surface.
- Put about 2 tablespoons of cooked pork on the lettuce then wrap it tightly. Place on a serving dish.
- Repeat with the remaining lettuce and pork then serve.
- Enjoy!

Per Serving: Net Carbs: 2.9g; Calories: 369; Total Fat: 31.5g; Saturated Fat: 13.4g
Protein: 16.2g; Carbs: 5.2g; Fiber: 2.1g; Sugar: 2g

Fat 77% / Protein 20% / Carbs 3%

Baked Lamb Ribs Rosemary

Serves: 4 / Preparation time: 9 minutes / Cooking time: 19 minutes

1-lb. lamb leg

3 tablespoons minced garlic

3 tablespoons extra virgin olive oil

¼ cup chopped rosemary

½ tablespoon pepper

- Preheat an oven to 375°F (190°C) and line a baking tray with aluminum foil.
- Rub the lamb leg with minced garlic and olive oil then sprinkle pepper over the lamb leg.
- Place the seasoned lamb leg on the prepared baking tray and sprinkle chopped rosemary over the lamb leg.
- Once the oven is ready, place the baking tray in the oven and bake the lamb leg for approximately 20 minutes or until the lamb leg is tender and cooked through.
- When the baked lamb leg is done, take it out from the oven and arrange on a serving dish
- Serve and enjoy warm.

Per Serving: Net Carbs: 3g; Calories: 413; Total Fat: 35.1g; Saturated Fat: 11.8g
Protein: 20.7g; Carbs: 4.9g; Fiber: 1.9g; Sugar: 0.1g

Fat 76% / Protein 21% / Carbs 3%

Oven Baked Lamb Ribs Macadamia with Tomato Salsa

Serves: 4 / Preparation time: 16 minutes / Cooking time: 21 minutes

¾ lb. lamb ribs

½ cup macadamia

1 teaspoon minced garlic

½ cup fresh parsley

4 tablespoons extra virgin olive oil

½ teaspoon pepper

1-cup cherry tomatoes

1-tablespoon macadamia oil

1-tablespoon balsamic vinegar

- Preheat an oven to 400°F (204°C) and line a baking tray with aluminum foil. Set aside.
- Cut the lamb ribs into medium pieces then set aside.
- Place the macadamia in a food processor then add minced garlic, fresh parsley, olive oil, and pepper to the food processor. Process until smooth.
- Coat the lamb ribs with the macadamia mixture then arrange on the prepared baking tray.
- Place the coated lamb ribs in the oven and bake for approximately 25 minutes or until the lamb is completely cooked.
- In the meantime, cut the cherry tomatoes into halves then place in a disposable aluminum cup.
- Drizzle macadamia oil over the tomatoes then toss to combine. Set aside.
- Once the lamb is done, remove from the oven and arrange on a serving dish.
- Next, place the tomatoes in the oven and bake for approximately 5 minutes.
- Remove the tomatoes from the oven and drizzle balsamic vinegar over the tomatoes. Stir well.
- Top the baked lamb with tomato salsa then serve.
- Enjoy warm.

Per Serving: Net Carbs: 3.1g; Calories: 486; Total Fat: 44.2g; Saturated Fat: 8.2g
Protein: 19.9g; Carbs: 6.1g; Fiber: 3g; Sugar: 2.4g

Fat 82% / Protein 15% / Carbs 3%

Grilled Lamb Shoulder with Creamy Mint Sauce

Serves: 4 / Preparation time: 2 hours / Cooking time: 22 minutes

1 lb. lamb shoulder

4 tablespoons extra virgin olive oil

½ teaspoon oregano

2 tablespoons wine

1-teaspoon rosemary

3 tablespoons chopped fresh dill

¼ cup chopped fresh mint leaves

1 tablespoon lemon juice

¼ cup coconut cream

- Rub the lamb shoulder with olive oil, oregano, wine, and rosemary then marinate for at least 2 hours. Store in the fridge to keep it fresh.
- In the meantime, place fresh dill, mint leaves, lemon juice and coconut cream in a food processor then process until smooth.
- Transfer the creamy sauce to a container with a lid and store in the refrigerator.
- After 2 hours, take the lamb shoulder out of the fridge and thaw at room temperature.
- Preheat a grill over medium heat then arrange the marinated lamb shoulder on it.
- Grill the lamb for approximately 10 minutes each side or until the lamb is completely cooked.
- Once it is done, remove the grilled lamb shoulder from the grill and place on a serving dish.
- Top with creamy mint sauce then serve immediately.
- Enjoy warm.

Per Serving: Net Carbs: 1.9g; Calories: 342; Total Fat: 26.8g; Saturated Fat: 8.3g
Protein: 23.1g; Carbs: 3.2g; Fiber: 1.3g; Sugar: 0.7g

Fat 70% / Protein 28% / Carbs 2%

Savory Lamb Garlic with Walnut Green Pesto

Serves: 4 / Preparation time: 11 minutes / Cooking time: 17 minutes

1-½ lbs. lamb chops

3 teaspoons minced garlic

½ teaspoon pepper

3 cups fresh basil

½ cup roasted walnuts

½ cup extra virgin olive oil

1 tablespoon lemon juice

- Preheat an oven to 400°F (204°C) and line a baking tray with aluminum foil.
- In the meantime, rub the lamb chops with minced garlic and pepper then set aside.
- Preheat a saucepan over medium heat then pour about a tablespoon of olive oil into the saucepan.
- Once the oil is hot, place the lamb chops in the saucepan then sauté until seared.
- After that, transfer the lamb chops to the prepared baking tray then place in the oven.
- Bake the lamb chop for 15 minutes or until it is completely cooked.
- Meanwhile, place fresh basil, roasted walnuts, lemon juice, and extra virgin olive to the food processor then process until smooth and creamy.
- When the lamb is done, remove from the oven and transfer to a serving dish.
- Top the lamb with basil and walnut mixture then serve.
- Enjoy!

Per Serving: Net Carbs: 1.5g; Calories: 491; Total Fat: 43.6g; Saturated Fat: 7.2g
Protein: 26.5g; Carbs: 3g; Fiber: 1.5g; Sugar: 0.3g

Fat 80% / Protein 19% / Carbs 1%

Lamb Meatballs with Cucumber Avocado-Creamy Sauce

Serves: 4 / Preparation time: 20 minutes / Cooking time: 34 minutes

1 lb. ground lamb

½ cup diced onion

2 teaspoons minced garlic

½ teaspoon grated lemon zest

½ teaspoon oregano

½ teaspoon coriander

½ teaspoon cumin

½ teaspoon pepper

1 ripe avocado

1 medium cucumber

1 tablespoon lemon juice

¼ cup Greek yogurt

- Preheat an oven 350°F (177°C) and line a baking tray with aluminum foil.
- Season ground lamb with onion, minced garlic, grated lemon zest, oregano, coriander, cumin, and pepper then mix well.
- Shape the mixture onto medium balls forms then arrange on the prepared baking tray.
- Bake the lamb balls for approximately 25 minutes or until set.
- Meanwhile, cut the avocado into halves then discard the seed.
- Scoop out the avocado flesh then place in a food processor.
- Next, peel the cucumber and discard the seeds.
- Cut the cucumber into cubes then add to the food processor.
- Pour lemon juice and yogurt to the food processor then process until smooth and creamy.
- Once the lamb balls are done, remove from the oven and transfer to a serving dish.
- Drizzle cucumber avocado sauce on top and serve immediately.
- Enjoy!

Per Serving: Net Carbs: 5.7g; Calories: 455; Total Fat: 37.2g; Saturated Fat: 14.3g
Protein: 22.3g; Carbs: 10g; Fiber: 4.3g; Sugar: 2.7g

Fat 74% / Protein 21% / Carbs 5%

Crunchy Crusted Pecan Of Goat

Serves: 4 / Preparation time: 9 minutes / Cooking time: 44 minutes

1 lb. goat leg

½ teaspoon pepper

3 tablespoons extra virgin olive oil

½ cup chopped onion

½ teaspoon grated lemon zest

1-cup ground pecans

1-tablespoon mustard

- Preheat an oven to 400°F (204°C) and line a baking tray with aluminum foil.
- Score the goat leg at several places then sprinkle pepper over the goat leg.
- Wait until the oven is ready then oven the goat leg for approximately 10 minutes.
- In the meantime, preheat a saucepan over medium heat then pour extra virgin olive oil into it.
- Once the oil is hot, stir in chopped onion and sauté until wilted and aromatic.
- After that, add ground pecans and grated lemon zest to the saucepan then stir well.
- Take the goat leg from the oven and coat with mustard.
- Top the goat leg with the pecan mixture then return to the oven and bake for approximately 35 minutes or until the goat leg is tender.
- Once it is done, remove the cooked goat leg from the oven and transfer to a serving dish.
- Serve and enjoy.

Per Serving: Net Carbs: 2.4g; Calories: 460; Total Fat: 40.1g; Saturated Fat: 11.9g
Protein: 21.5g; Carbs: 3.8g; Fiber: 1.4g; Sugar: 0.8g

Fat 78% / Protein 20% / Carbs 2%

Spicy Turmeric Goat Satay

Serves: 4 / Preparation time: 9 minutes / Cooking time: 29 minutes

1 lb. ground goat meat

½ cup diced onion

2 teaspoons grated garlic

1-teaspoon turmeric

2 teaspoons red chili flakes

1 egg

- Preheat a steamer over medium heat and wait until it is ready.
- Season the ground goat meat with diced onion, grated garlic, turmeric, and red chili flakes then mix well.
- Crack the egg then add to the seasoned goat meat mixture then mix until combined.
- Take half of a handful of the mixture then mold the meat mixture around a wooden skewer. Repeat with the remaining goat meat.
- Arrange the satay in the steamer and steam for approximately 20 minutes or until set.
- Once the satay is done, remove from the steamer and let it rest for a few minutes.
- Next, preheat a grill over medium heat and once it is done, arrange the satay on the grill and grill for about 3 minutes each side or until both sides of the satay are lightly golden brown.
- Arrange the grilled satay on a serving dish then serve.
- Enjoy warm.

Per Serving: Net Carbs: 3.4g; Calories: 355; Total Fat: 28.3g; Saturated Fat: 12.4g
Protein: 21.1g; Carbs: 4.2g; Fiber: 0.8g; Sugar: 1.9g

Fat 77% / Protein 19% / Carbs 4%

Coconut Creamy Goat Fritters with Sautéed Eggplant

Serves: 4 / Preparation time: 19 minutes / Cooking time: 14 minutes

1 lb. ground goat meat

½ cup chopped leek

2 teaspoons minced garlic

1 egg

4 tablespoons extra virgin olive oil

½ teaspoon pepper

1 cup cubed eggplant

¼ cup coconut milk

½ tablespoon coconut flour

1 tablespoons lemon

- Season the ground goat meat with minced garlic and pepper then combine with egg. Mix well.
- Add chopped leek to the meat and mix until just combined.
- Shape the meat mixture into medium fritters then set aside.
- Next, preheat a saucepan over medium heat then pour extra virgin olive oil into it.
- Once the oil is hot, put the fritters on the saucepan. Don't be too close.
- Cook the fritters for approximately 3 minutes each side or until the fritters are lightly golden brown and cooked through.
- Remove the fritters from the pan and arrange on a serving dish.
- After that, put the cubed eggplant into the pan and sauté with the remaining olive oil until just wilted.
- Remove the eggplant from heat and place next to the fritters.
- Keep the saucepan over medium heat then pour the coconut flour and coconut mixture into the saucepan. Bring to a simmer.
- Once it is done, remove from heat and add lemon to the sauce.
- Drizzle the coconut sauce over the fritters and eggplants then serve.
- Enjoy!

Per Serving: Net Carbs: 3.8g; Calories: 513; Total Fat: 46g; Saturated Fat: 17.8g
Protein: 21.5g; Carbs: 5.5g; Fiber: 1.7g; Sugar: 1.8g

Fat 81% / Protein 16% / Carbs 3%

Gingery Baked Goat Curry with Cauliflower

Serves: 4 / Preparation time: 12 minutes / Cooking time: 44 minutes

¾ lb. goat meat

4 tablespoons extra virgin olive oil

1-teaspoon ginger

½ teaspoon cumin

1-teaspoon cilantro

¾ teaspoon turmeric

1 cup chopped onion

2 cups cauliflower florets

½ teaspoon pepper

¾ cup coconut milk

1-tablespoon curry

- Preheat an oven to 350°F (177°C) and prepare a disposable aluminum pan. Set aside.
- Place ginger, cumin, cilantro, and turmeric in a bowl then pour olive oil over the spices. Stir until incorporated.
- Cut the goat meat into cubes then rub with the olive oil mixture.
- Place the seasoned goat meat in the prepared aluminum pan then sprinkle chopped onion over the goat meat.
- Bake the goat meat for approximately 30 minutes or until tender.
- In the meantime, combine coconut milk, curry, and pepper in a saucepan then bring to a simmer. Remove from heat.
- After 30 minutes, take the aluminum pan out of the oven and sprinkle cauliflower florets over the goat meat.
- Drizzle coconut sauce on top then cover the aluminum pan with aluminum foil.
- Return the aluminum pan to the oven and bake for about 15 minutes.
- Once it is done, remove the aluminum pan from the oven and let it rest for a few minutes.
- Discard the cover then transfer the cooked goat meat to a serving dish together with the cauliflower.
- Serve and enjoy.

Per Serving: Net Carbs: 6g; Calories: 339; Total Fat: 26.9g; Saturated Fat: 12.1g
Protein: 18.4g; Carbs: 9.6g; Fiber: 3.6g; Sugar: 4g

Fat 71% / Protein 22% / Carbs 7%

Minty Goat Roll with Roasted Broccoli and Carrots

Serves: 4 / Preparation time: 12 minutes / Cooking time: 38 minutes

¾ lb. goat meat

1-teaspoon pepper

1-teaspoon thyme

1-teaspoon sage

1-teaspoon rosemary

3 teaspoons minced garlic

½ teaspoon grated lemon zest

½ cup extra virgin olive oil

½ cup chopped mint leaves

¼ cup chopped parsley

1 tablespoon lemon juice

1-cup broccoli florets

1 cup chopped carrots

½ cup diced onion

- Preheat an oven to 350°F (177°C) and prepare a disposable aluminum pan. Set aside.
- Combine ¼ cup of olive oil with pepper, thyme, sage, rosemary, minced garlic, and grated lemon zest then stir until incorporated.
- Cut the goat meat into thin slices then rub with the spice mixture. Let it rest for a few minutes.
- Next, combine chopped mint leaves with parsley then pour the remaining olive oil and lemon juice over the greens. Mix well.
- Arrange the sliced meat on a flat surface then put the mint leaves mixture on top.
- Roll the goat meat and tightly bind with string.
- Spread broccoli florets, chopped carrots, and diced onion in the prepared aluminum pan then place the rolled goat meat on it.
- Place the aluminum pan in the oven and bake for approximately 40 minutes or until the goat meat is tender and cooked through.
- Once it is done, remove the aluminum pan from the oven let it rest for a few minutes.
- Take the rolled goat meat out of the aluminum pan and place on a flat surface.
- Cut the rolled goat meat into thick slices and arrange on a serving dish.
- Top with the roasted vegetables then serve.
- Enjoy!

Per Serving: Net Carbs: 5.4g; Calories: 337; Total Fat: 27.3g; Saturated Fat: 4.2g
Protein: 17.6g; Carbs: 8.4g; Fiber: 3g; Sugar: 2.5g

Fat 72% / Protein 22% / Carbs 6%

POULTRY

Contents

Coconut Creamy Chicken Cheese

Serves: 4 / Preparation time: 12 minutes / Cooking time: 14 minutes

¾ lb. boneless chicken thighs

2-½ tablespoons extra virgin olive oil

¼ cup coconut milk

¾ cup chicken broth

2 teaspoons minced garlic

1 ½ teaspoons Italian seasoning

½ cup grated Parmesan cheese

1 ½ cup chopped spinach

½ cup halved cherry tomatoes

- Cut the boneless chicken thighs into medium pieces then set aside.
- Preheat a skillet over medium heat then pour extra virgin olive oil into it.
- Once the oil is hot, stir in minced garlic then sauté until lightly golden and aromatic.
- Next, add the boneless chicken thighs to the skillet then stir until wilted.
- Pour chicken broth over the chicken then bring to boil.
- Once it is boiled, reduce the heat and cook until the chicken is completely done.
- Pour coconut milk over the chicken and season the chicken with Italian seasoning.
- Once it is done, add chopped spinach and cherry tomatoes to the skillet. Stir until just wilted.
- Transfer the cooked chicken together with the gravy and vegetables to a serving dish then quickly sprinkle grated Parmesan cheese on top. Stir well.
- Serve and enjoy warm.

Per Serving: Net Carbs: 3.5g; Calories: 432; Total Fat: 42.7g; Saturated Fat: 20.6g
Protein: 10.6g; Carbs: 4.1g; Fiber: 0.6g; Sugar: 3.2g

Fat 72% / Protein 25% / Carbs 3%

Spicy Chicken Turmeric

Serves: 4 / Preparation time: 8 minutes / Cooking time: 16 minutes

¾ lb. boneless chicken thighs

2 tablespoons lemon juice

2 tablespoons extra virgin olive oil

2 cloves garlic

3 shallots

2 tablespoons red chili flakes

2 teaspoons cayenne

½ teaspoon turmeric

2 kaffir lime leaves

2 bay leaves

2 cups water

- Drizzle lemon juice over the chicken thighs then let it rest for approximately 10 minutes.
- In the meantime, place garlic, shallots, red chili flakes, and cayenne in a food processor then process until smooth.
- Next, preheat a skillet over medium heat then pour extra virgin olive oil into it.
- Once the oil is hot, stir in the spice mixture and sauté until aromatic.
- After that, add chicken to the skillet and stir until the chicken is no longer pink.
- Season the chicken with kaffir lime leaves and bay leaves then pour water over the chicken. Bring to boil.
- Once it is boiled, reduce the heat and cook until the chicken is completely seasoned and cooked through.
- Transfer the cooked chicken together with the gravy to a serving dish and serve.
- Enjoy!

Per Serving: Net Carbs: 5.5g; Calories: 268; Total Fat: 20.2g; Saturated Fat: 4.9g
Protein: 15.9g; Carbs: 6.3g; Fiber: 0.6g; Sugar: 1.5g

Fat 70% / Protein 22% / Carbs 8%

Crispy Chicken Oregano with Coconut Coating

Serves: 4 / Preparation time: 8 minutes / Cooking time: 14 minutes

½ lb. boneless chicken thigh

2 eggs

½ teaspoon oregano

½ teaspoon pepper

¼ cup almond flour

1 cup grated coconut

1-cup extra virgin olive oil, to fry

- Cut the chicken thigh into slices then set aside.
- Crack the eggs then place the eggs in a bowl.
- Season the eggs with pepper and oregano then stir well.
- Next, add almond flour to the seasoned eggs then mix until combined.
- Dip the sliced chicken into the egg mixture then roll in the grated coconut. Make sure that the chicken is completely coated with the grated coconut.
- Preheat a frying pan over medium heat then pour extra virgin olive oil into it.
- Put the coated chicken into the frying pan then fry until both sides are lightly golden brown and the chicken is completely cooked.
- Once it is done, remove the chicken from the frying pan strain the oil.
- Arrange on a serving dish and serve the chicken warm.
- Enjoy immediately.

Per Serving: Net Carbs: 1.5g; Calories: 464; Total Fat: 45.5g; Saturated Fat: 13.1g
Protein: 13.5g; Carbs: 3.4g; Fiber: 1.9g; Sugar: 1.4g

Fat 88% / Protein 19% / Carbs 1%

Chicken Tomato Soup with Mushroom

Serves: 4 / Preparation time: 6 minutes / Cooking time: 22 minutes

¾ lb. boneless chicken thigh

2 tablespoons extra virgin olive oil

½ cup chopped onion

2 cups water

½ cup tomato puree

½ teaspoon pepper

¼ teaspoon nutmeg

½ cup chopped mushroom

2 tablespoons chopped celeries

- Cut the boneless chicken thigh into small pieces then set aside.
- Preheat a skillet over medium heat then pour extra virgin olive oil into it.
- Once the oil is hot, stir in chopped onion and sauté until aromatic and lightly golden brown.
- Add chicken to the skillet then sauté until just wilted.
- Pour water over the chicken then season the soup with pepper and nutmeg. Stir well then bring to boil.
- Once it is boiled, reduce the heat and cook the soup for about 10 minutes or until the chicken is completely seasoned.
- Pour tomato puree over the chicken and add chopped mushroom to the soup. Bring to a simmer.
- Once it is done, transfer the chicken soup to a serving bowl then sprinkle chopped celeries on top.
- Serve and enjoy warm.

Per Serving: Net Carbs: 3.4g; Calories: 202; Total Fat: 15.6g; Saturated Fat: 3.5g
Protein: 11g; Carbs: 4.5g; Fiber: 1.1g; Sugar: 2.4g

Fat 70% / Protein 23% / Carbs 7%

Chicken Cheese Balls with Coconut Crumbles

Serves: 4 / Preparation time: 4 minutes / Cooking time: 26 minutes

1 lb. boneless chicken thigh

½ cup grated cheddar cheese

2 eggs

2 tablespoons almond flour

¼ teaspoon pepper

1 cup grated coconut

½ cup extra virgin olive oil, to fry

- Cut the boneless chicken thigh then put in a food processor. Process until smooth.
- Transfer the chicken to a mixing bowl then add almond flour to the chicken.
- Crack an egg and drop in the bowl and after that, mix the chicken with the almond flour and egg until combined.
- Shape the chicken mixture into small balls then set aside.
- Crack the remaining egg and place in a bowl.
- Season the egg with pepper then mix well.
- Next, dip each chicken ball in the egg mixture then roll in the grated coconut. Make sure that the cheese balls are completely coated with grated coconut.
- After that, preheat a frying pan over medium heat then pour olive oil into it.
- Once the oil is hot, carefully put the chicken cheese balls in the skillet and fry until all sides are lightly golden brown and crispy.
- Remove the fried chicken cheese balls from the frying pan then strain the oil.
- Arrange the cheese balls on a serving dish and serve.
- Enjoy immediately.

Per Serving: Net Carbs: 1.3g; Calories: 592; Total Fat: 53.9g; Saturated Fat: 16.7g
Protein: 25.4g; Carbs: 3.6g; Fiber: 1.9g; Sugar: 1.5g

Fat 82% / Protein 17% / Carbs 1%

Grilled Chicken Satay with Spicy Cashew Sauces

Serves: 4 / Preparation time: 4 minutes / Cooking time: 19 minutes

1-¼ lbs. boneless chicken thighs

½ teaspoon pepper

3 tablespoons extra virgin olive oil

¼ cup roasted cashews

2 tablespoons red chili flakes

¼ cup water

2 tablespoons coconut aminos

1 teaspoon minced garlic

1 kaffir lime leaf

- Cut the boneless chicken thighs into cubes then season with pepper. Let the chicken rest
- Place roasted cashews in a blender then add red chili flakes and minced garlic to the blender.
- Pour water into over the cashews then blend until smooth.
- Transfer the cashew mixture to a saucepan then add kaffir lime leaf to it. Bring to a simmer.
- Once it is done, remove the cashew sauce from heat then drizzle coconut aminos over the sauce. Stir well then let it cool.
- Next, preheat a grill over medium heat then wait until it is ready.
- In the meantime, using a wooden skewer prick the chicken cubes then brush with extra virgin olive oil.
- Once the grill is ready, place the chicken satay on it and grill until done. Don't forget to flip the chicken satay and make sure that both sides of the chicken satay are completely cooked.
- Arrange the cooked chicken satay on a serving dish then drizzle cashew sauce on top.
- Serve and enjoy warm.

Per Serving: Net Carbs: 4.3g; Calories: 451; Total Fat: 33.2g; Saturated Fat: 8.8g
Protein: 32.1g; Carbs: 5g; Fiber: 0.7g; Sugar: 1.7g

Fat 73% / Protein 23% / Carbs 4%

Cheesy Chicken Loaf with Broccoli and Carrot

Serves: 4 / Preparation time: 9 minutes / Cooking time: 19 minutes

1-¼ lbs. boneless chicken thighs

2 eggs

3 tablespoons extra virgin olive oil

½ cup chopped onion

½ teaspoon pepper

½ cup chopped broccoli

½ lb. carrots

1-cup cheddar cheese cubes

- Preheat a steamer and prepare a loaf pan. Coat with cooking spray and set aside.
- Peel the carrots and cut into small dices. Set aside.
- Cut the boneless chicken thigh into cubes then place in a food processor. Process until smooth then set aside.
- Next, preheat a saucepan over medium heat then pour olive oil into it.
- Once the oil is hot, stir in chopped onion and sauté until wilted and aromatic. Remove from heat.
- Combine the chicken with eggs then season with pepper.
- Add sautéed onion, chopped broccoli, carrots, and cheese cubes to the chicken mixture then mix well.
- Transfer the chicken mixture to the prepared loaf pan then spread evenly.
- Place the loaf pan in the steamer and steam the chicken loaf for approximately 20 minutes.
- Once the chicken loaf is done, remove from the steamer and let it cool for a few minutes.
- Take the chicken loaf out of the pan then let it cool for about 10 minutes.
- Cut the chicken loaf into thick slices then arrange on a serving dish.
- Serve and enjoy!

Per Serving: Net Carbs: 6.2g; Calories: 433; Total Fat: 33.8g; Saturated Fat: 11.6g
Protein: 24.4g; Carbs: 8.3g; Fiber: 2.1g; Sugar: 3.8g

Fat 70% / Protein 24% / Carbs 6%

Crispy Almond Chicken with Tomato Onion Sauce

Serves: 4 / Preparation time: 11 minutes / Cooking time: 21 minutes

¾ lb. boneless chicken thighs

1 egg

¼ cup almond flour

½ cup extra virgin olive oil, to fry

1 cup chopped onion

½ cup tomato puree

¼ teaspoon pepper

- Cut the boneless chicken thighs into thin slices then set aside.
- Crack the egg then place in a bowl. Beat until incorporated.
- Next, dip the sliced chicken in the beaten egg then roll in the almond flour. Repeat with the remaining chicken and almond flour.
- After that, preheat a pan over medium heat then pour olive oil into it.
- Once the oil is hot, put the coated chicken into the pan then fry until both sides are lightly golden brown and the chicken is cooked through.
- Remove the cooked chicken from the pan and discard the excessive oil.
- Arrange the fried chicken on a serving dish then set aside.
- Take 2 tablespoons of oil then pour into a saucepan.
- Stir in chopped onion then sauté until lightly golden brown and aromatic.
- Next, add tomato puree to the saucepan then season with pepper. Stir well and bring to a simmer.
- Once it is done, remove the sauce from heat then drizzle the tomato sauce over the chicken.
- Serve and enjoy warm.

Per Serving: Net Carbs: 2.8g; Calories: 433; Total Fat: 40g; Saturated Fat: 7.8g
Protein: 17.2g; Carbs: 3.7g; Fiber: 0.9g; Sugar: 1.4g

Fat 83% / Protein 14% / Carbs 3%

Marinated Chicken Lemon Jalapeno

Serves: 4 / Preparation time: 11 minutes / Cooking time: 2 hours 19 minutes

1-½ lbs. chicken thighs

4 tablespoons extra virgin olive oil

2 cups chopped onion

2 tablespoons minced garlic

3 tablespoons chopped jalapeno

3 tablespoons lemon juice

2 teaspoons thyme

1-teaspoon cinnamon

- Combine extra virgin olive oil with lemon juice then season with onion, jalapeno, minced garlic, thyme, and cinnamon. Stir well.
- Rub the chicken thighs with the spice mixture then marinate for approximately 2 hours. Store in the fridge to keep it fresh.
- After 2 hours, remove the marinated chicken from the fridge and thaw at room temperature.
- In the meantime, preheat a grill over medium heat then wait until it is ready.
- Place the marinated chicken thighs on the grill and grill for approximately 20 minutes or until cooked through. Occasionally, brush the chicken thighs with the remaining marinade.
- Once it is done, remove the grilled chicken thighs from the grill and arrange on a serving dish.
- Serve and enjoy.

Per Serving: Net Carbs: 6g; Calories: 396; Total Fat: 31.3g; Saturated Fat: 7.1g
Protein: 21.1g; Carbs: 8g; Fiber: 2g; Sugar: 2.9g

Fat 71% / Protein 23% / Carbs 6%

Tomato Chicken Stew with Baby Spinach

Serves: 4 / Preparation time: 9 minutes / Cooking time: 41 minutes

1 lb. chopped boneless chicken thighs

3 tablespoons extra virgin olive oil

2 tablespoons minced garlic

½ teaspoon oregano

½ teaspoon pepper

½ cup halved cherry tomatoes

1-cup water

½ cup coconut milk

1 cup chopped baby spinach

- Preheat a skillet over medium heat then pour extra virgin olive oil into it.
- Once it is hot, stir in minced garlic then sauté until lightly golden and aromatic.
- Next, add chopped boneless chicken thighs to the skillet and sauté until the chicken is no longer pink.
- Season the chicken with oregano and pepper then pour water over the chicken. Bring to boil.
- Once it is boiled, reduce the heat and cook until the chicken is tender and the water is completely absorbed into the chicken.
- Pour coconut milk into the skillet and add halved cherry tomatoes to the stew. Bring to a simmer.
- Once it is done, add chopped baby spinach to the skillet and stir well.
- Remove the chicken stew from heat and transfer to a serving dish.
- Serve and enjoy warm.

Per Serving: Net Carbs: 2.8g; Calories: 410; Total Fat: 34.8g; Saturated Fat: 12.9g
Protein: 21.3g; Carbs: 4g; Fiber: 1.2g; Sugar: 1.1g

Fat 76% / Protein 21% / Carbs 3%

Grilled Chicken Thighs Rosemary

Serves: 4 / Preparation time: 11 minutes / Cooking time: 39 minutes

1-½ lbs. chicken thighs

3 tablespoons balsamic vinegar

3 tablespoons extra virgin olive oil

3 tablespoons minced garlic

1-½ teaspoons thyme

2 teaspoons chopped rosemary

½ teaspoon pepper

- Combine balsamic vinegar with extra virgin olive oil then season with minced garlic, thyme, pepper, and chopped rosemary.
- Rub the chicken thighs with the spice mixture then let it rest for approximately 15 minutes.
- In the meantime, preheat a grill over medium heat then wait until it is ready.
- Place the seasoned chicken thighs on the grill then grill until all sides of the chicken are golden brown and cooked through. Brush the chicken thighs with the marinade once every 5 minutes.
- Once it is done, remove the chicken from the grill and transfer to a serving dish.
- Serve and enjoy warm.

Per Serving: Net Carbs: 2.3g; Calories: 465; Total Fat: 36.2g; Saturated Fat: 9.1g
Protein: 30.5g; Carbs: 2.9g; Fiber: 0.6g; Sugar: 0.1g

Fat 70% / Protein 28% / Carbs 2%

Cheesy Chicken Zucchini in Savory Coconut Gravy

Serves: 4 / Preparation time: 11 minutes / Cooking time: 34 minutes

1 lb. boneless chicken thighs

2 tablespoons extra virgin olive oil

2 tablespoons minced garlic

½ teaspoon black pepper

1 teaspoon Italian seasoning

½ cup coconut milk

1 cup sliced zucchini

¾ cup grated cheddar cheese

¼ cup chopped parsley

- Cut the boneless chicken thighs into cubes then set aside.
- Next, preheat a skillet over medium heat then pour extra virgin olive oil into it.
- Once the oil is hot, add chicken cubes to the skillet and sauté until wilted. Cook until the chicken is done.
- Remove the cooked chicken from the skillet and place on a plate.
- Next, stir in minced garlic to the skillet then sauté until lightly golden brown and aromatic.
- After that, pour coconut milk into the skillet and season with black pepper and Italian seasoning. Bring to a simmer.
- Once it is done, put the cooked chicken and sliced zucchini to the skillet and stir until the chicken is completely coated with the seasoned coconut milk.
- Transfer the cooked chicken and the gravy to a serving dish then sprinkle grated cheddar cheese on top.
- Garnish with fresh parsley and serve.
- Enjoy immediately.

Per Serving: Net Carbs: 3.5g; Calories: 471; Total Fat: 38.6g; Saturated Fat: 16.9g
Protein: 26.7g; Carbs: 4.8g; Fiber: 1.3g; Sugar: 1.8g

Fat 74% / Protein 23% / Carbs 3%

Garlicky Chicken Asparagus

Serves: 4 / Preparation time: 11 minutes / Cooking time: 39 minutes

1-½ lbs. boneless chicken thighs

3 tablespoons extra virgin olive oil

2 tablespoons lemon juice

3 tablespoons minced garlic

¾ teaspoon oregano

½ teaspoon black pepper

½ lb. chopped asparagus

1 fresh lemon

- Preheat an oven to 250°F (121°C) and line a baking tray with parchment paper.
- Next, cut the boneless chicken thighs into medium cubes then set aside.
- Combine extra virgin olive oil with lemon juice, minced garlic, oregano, and black pepper then mix well.
- Rub the boneless chicken thighs with the spice mixture then spread on the prepared baking tray.
- Sprinkle asparagus over the chicken then arrange sliced lemon on top.
- Bake the chicken for approximately 25 minutes or until the chicken is cooked through.
- Once it is done, remove the cooked chicken from the oven and transfer to a serving dish.
- Serve and enjoy.

Per Serving: Net Carbs: 3.5g; Calories: 470; Total Fat: 36.2g; Saturated Fat: 9.1g
Protein: 31.1g; Carbs: 4.6g; Fiber: 1.1g; Sugar: 0.9g

Fat 70% / Protein 27% / Carbs 3%

Crispy Chicken with Cheese Sauce

Serves: 4 / Preparation time: 9 minutes / Cooking time: 41 minutes

1 lb. boneless chicken thigh

½ teaspoon black pepper

1 cup almond flour

1 egg

½ cup extra virgin olive oil, to fry

1 cup almond yogurt

1 cup grated cheddar cheese

2 teaspoons mustard

- Cut the boneless chicken thigh into slices then set aside.
- Crack the egg then place in a bowl.
- Season the egg with black pepper then stir until incorporated.
- Dip the sliced chicken in the beaten egg then roll in the almond flour. Make sure that the chicken is completely coated with almond flour.
- Preheat a frying pan over medium heat then pour olive oil into the pan.
- Once the oil is hot, put the chicken in the frying pan and fry until both sides of the chicken are lightly golden brown and the chicken is completely cooked.
- Remove the fried chicken from the frying pan and let it rest for a few minutes to discard the excessive oil. Place the crispy chicken on a serving dish.
- In the meantime, place almond yogurt, grated cheddar cheese, and mustard in a saucepan then bring to a simmer over very low heat.
- Stir the sauce until incorporated then remove from heat.
- Drizzle the cheese sauce over the chicken then serve.
- Enjoy warm!

Per Serving: Net Carbs: 4.5g; Calories: 439; Total Fat: 42.2g; Saturated Fat: 10.7g
Protein: 12.7g; Carbs: 5.6g; Fiber: 1.1g; Sugar: 3.4g

Fat 87% / Protein 9% / Carbs 4%

Sticky Chicken with Spicy Sauce

Serves: 4 / Preparation time: 12 minutes / Cooking time: 29 minutes

1-½ lbs. boneless chicken thighs

2 tablespoons lemon juice

4 tablespoons extra virgin olive oil

½ cup chopped onion

2 tablespoons diced green chili

1-tablespoon chili powder

1-tablespoon sweet paprika

1-teaspoon cumin

½ teaspoon oregano

3 tablespoons tomato puree

- Preheat an oven to 250°F (121°C) and line a baking tray with aluminum foil. Set aside.
- Cut the boneless chicken thighs into slices then rub with 2 tablespoons of extra virgin olive oil and lemon juice.
- Spread the chicken on the prepared baking tray then set aside.
- Next, preheat a saucepan over medium heat then pour the remaining olive oil into it.
- Once the oil is hot, stir in chopped onion and sauté until aromatic and lightly golden brown.
- After that, add tomato puree into the saucepan then season with diced green chili, chili powder, sweet paprika, cumin, and oregano. Stir well.
- Drizzle the sauce over the chicken then cover with aluminum foil.
- Place the baking tray in the preheated oven and bake the chicken for approximately 30 minutes or until the chicken is cooked through.
- Once it is done, remove the cooked chicken from the oven and let it rest for a few minutes.
- Unwrap the cooked chicken and transfer to a serving dish.
- Drizzle the remaining liquid over the chicken then serve.
- Enjoy warm.

Per Serving: Net Carbs: 3.2g; Calories: 386; Total Fat: 31.7g; Saturated Fat: 7.1g
Protein: 21g; Carbs: 5.2g; Fiber: 2g; Sugar: 1.8g

Fat 74% / Protein 23% / Carbs 3%

Savory Chicken Turmeric with Creamy Coconut Lemon Sauce

Serves: 4 / Preparation time: 11 minutes / Cooking time: 31 minutes

1 lb. boneless chicken thighs
2 tablespoons extra virgin olive oil
2 teaspoons minced garlic
½ teaspoon turmeric
1 lemon grass
2 tablespoons coconut oil

¼ cup chopped onion
2 tablespoons lemon juice
¾ cup chicken broth
¼ cup coconut milk
1-tablespoon coconut flour

- Cut the boneless chicken thighs into cubes then set aside.
- Preheat a skillet over medium heat then pour extra virgin olive oil into the skillet.
- Once the oil is hot, stir in minced garlic and sauté until lightly golden brown and aromatic.
- Add chicken cubes to the skillet then season with turmeric and lemon grass.
- Pour ½ cup chicken broth over the chicken cubes then bring to boil.
- Once it is boiled, reduced the heat and cook until the liquid is completely absorbed into the chicken.
- In the meantime, preheat a saucepan over medium heat then pour coconut oil into the pan.
- Stir in chopped onion then sauté until wilted and lightly golden brown.
- After that, reduce the heat and pour coconut milk into the saucepan.
- Combine chicken broth with coconut flour then stir well.
- Next, pour the chicken broth mixture to the saucepan then stir until incorporated. Bring to a simmer.
- Once it is done, remove the sauce from heat and drizzle lemon juice over the sauce. Stir well and set aside.
- Go back to the chicken and when it is done, remove the chicken from heat and transfer to a serving dish.
- Drizzle the lemon sauce over the chicken then serve.
- You can also serve the lemon sauce in a separated bowl.
- Enjoy warm!

Per Serving: Net Carbs: 2.8g; Calories: 420; Total Fat: 35.1g; Saturated Fat: 15.6g
Protein: 21.4g; Carbs: 4.7g; Fiber: 1.9g; Sugar: 1.3g

Fat 75% / Protein 22% / Carbs 3%

Broken Fried Duck with Green Chili Topping and Fried Cabbage

Serves: 4 / Preparation time: 14 minutes / Cooking time: 34 minutes

1 ½ lbs. bone-in duck thighs

3 tablespoons lemon juice

4 tablespoons minced garlic

1-teaspoon ginger

2 lemon grasses

1 bay leaf

2 cups water

2 cups chopped cabbage

½ cup extra virgin olive oil, to fry

2 tablespoons chopped green chili

- Rub the duck with lemon juice then let it rest for approximately 10 minutes.
- After 10 minutes, place the duck in a skillet then season with 3 tablespoons of minced garlic, ginger, lemon grasses, and bay leaf.
- Pour water over the duck then bring to boil.
- Once it is boiled, reduce the heat and cook until the water is completely absorbed into the duck.
- Once it is done, remove the duck from heat and set aside.
- Preheat a frying pan over medium heat and pour olive oil into the pan.
- Once the oil is hot, put the cooked duck in the frying pan and fry until both sides of the duck are lightly golden brown.
- Remove the fried duck from the frying pan and discard the excessive oil.
- Place the fried duck on a mortar then press until broken.
- Arrange the fried duck on a serving dish then set aside.
- Next, quickly fry the chopped cabbage then place next to the fried duck.
- After that, place green chili, the remaining minced garlic, and a teaspoon of olive oil in a food processor then process until smooth.
- Top the duck with green chili mixture then serve.
- Enjoy immediately.

Per Serving: Net Carbs: 5.4g; Calories: 436; Total Fat: 39g; Saturated Fat: 18.2g
Protein: 16.8g; Carbs: 6.6g; Fiber: 1.2g; Sugar: 1.7g

Fat 81% / Protein 14% / Carbs 5%

Spicy Duck with Steamed Green Collard

Serves: 4 / Preparation time: 16 minutes / Cooking time: 41 minutes

1 ½ lbs. bone-in duck thighs	3 tablespoons red chili flakes
2 tablespoons extra virgin olive oil	1 kaffir lime leaf
2 tablespoons minced garlic	2 cups water
2 teaspoons sliced shallots	½ cup coconut milk
1-teaspoon turmeric	1 cup chopped collard green

- Preheat a steamer over medium heat then steam the collard green until just tender.
- Remove the steamed collard green from heat then set aside.
- Preheat a skillet over medium heat then pour olive oil into it.
- Once the oil is hot, stir in minced garlic and sliced shallots then sauté until wilted and aromatic.
- Next, add the duck to the skillet and season with turmeric, red chili flakes, and kaffir lime leaves.
- After that, pour water over the duck then bring to boil.
- Once it is boiled, reduce the heat and cook until the duck is tender and cooked through.
- Pour coconut milk into the skillet then bring to a simmer. Occasionally stir the gravy until incorporated.
- When it is done, remove the cooked duck and the gravy to a serving bowl serve with steamed collard green.
- Enjoy!

Per Serving: Net Carbs: 6.7g; Calories: 353; Total Fat: 28.2g; Saturated Fat: 12g
Protein: 17.9g; Carbs: 8.9g; Fiber: 2.2g; Sugar: 3.1g

Fat 72% / Protein 20% / Carbs 8%

Tomato Chili Chicken Tender with Fresh Basils

Serves: 4 / Preparation time: 14 minutes / Cooking time: 31 minutes

1-¼ lbs. boneless chicken thighs

2 tablespoons minced garlic

2 lemon grasses

2 cups water

¼ cup diced red tomatoes

2 tablespoons red chili flakes

3 tablespoons extra virgin olive oil

½ cup fresh basils

- Cut the boneless chicken thighs into medium cubes then place in a skillet.
- Season the chicken with minced garlic and lemon grasses then pour water over the chicken. Bring to boil.
- Once it is boiled, reduce the heat and cook until the water is completely absorbed into the chicken.
- Remove the cooked chicken from heat then set aside.
- Next, preheat a saucepan over medium heat then pour olive oil into it.
- Once the oil is hot, stir in the chicken and cook until lightly brown.
- Add red tomatoes, red chili flakes, and fresh basils to the saucepan then stir until wilted and the chicken is completely seasoned.
- Transfer the chicken to a serving dish then serve.
- Enjoy!

Per Serving: Net Carbs: 3.9g; Calories: 410; Total Fat: 31.9g; Saturated Fat: 7.8g
Protein: 25.9g; Carbs: 4.5g; Fiber: 0.6g; Sugar: 1.5g

Fat 70% / Protein 26% / Carbs 4%

Chicken Avocado Creamy Salad

Serves: 4 / Preparation time: 11 minutes / Cooking time: 29 minutes

1 lb. boneless chicken thighs

½ cup almond milk

1-teaspoon oregano

2 tablespoons lemon juice

3 tablespoons extra virgin olive oil

1 ripe avocado

2 tablespoons chopped celeries

2 tablespoons cilantro

¼ cup diced onion

¼ teaspoon pepper

- Add oregano to the almond milk then stir well.
- Cut the boneless chicken thighs into slices then rub with almond milk mixture. Let it rest for approximately 10 minutes.
- In the meantime, preheat an oven to 250°F (121°C) and line a baking tray with aluminum foil.
- Once the oven is ready, spread the seasoned chicken on the prepared baking tray and bake for approximately 20 minutes or until the chicken is done.
- While waiting for the chicken, cut the avocado into halves then remove the seed.
- Peel the avocado then cut into cubes.
- Place the avocado cubes in a salad bowl then drizzle lemon juice and extra virgin olive oil over the avocado.
- Add chopped celeries, cilantro, onion, and pepper to the salad bowl then toss to combine.
- Once the chicken is done, remove from the oven and transfer to a serving dish.
- Top the chicken with avocado salad then serve immediately.
- Enjoy right away.

Per Serving: Net Carbs: 2.8g; Calories: 448; Total Fat: 40.3g; Saturated Fat: 13.7g
Protein: 16.9g; Carbs: 7.3g; Fiber: 4.5g; Sugar: 1.8g

Fat 81% / Protein 16% / Carbs 3%

SEAFOOD

Contents

Grilled Salmon Garlic with Tahini Sauce

Serves: 4 / Preparation time: 14 minutes / Cooking time: 12 minutes

1 ½ lbs. salmon

1 fresh lime

10 cloves garlic

¼ cup extra virgin olive oil

1-teaspoon cumin

¾ teaspoon coriander

1 ½ teaspoons paprika

½ teaspoon black pepper

3 tablespoons tahini paste

¼ cup water

1 tablespoon lemon juice

¼ teaspoon garlic powder

¾ cup chopped parsley

- Cut the lime into halves then squeeze the juice over the salmon. Let the salmon rest for approximately 10 minutes.
- In the meantime, place garlic cloves in a food processor then add extra virgin olive oil, cumin, coriander, paprika, and black pepper to the food processor. Process until smooth.
- Wash and rinse the salmon then pat it dry.
- Rub the salmon with the garlic mixture then set aside.
- Next, prepare a grill and preheat it to medium heat.
- Once the grill is ready, place the seasoned salmon directly on the grill and grill for approximately 5 minutes each side.
- Once it is done, remove the grilled salmon from the grill and transfer to a serving dish.
- Place tahini paste and garlic powder in a food processor then pour water and lemon juice over the paste. Process until smooth.
- Transfer the tahini sauce to a serving bowl then add chopped parsley to the sauce. Mix well.
- Serve the grilled salmon with tahini sauce and enjoy warm.

Per Serving: Net Carbs: 5.9g; Calories: 298; Total Fat: 24.5g; Saturated Fat: 3.7g
Protein: 15.1g; Carbs: 8.4g; Fiber: 2.5g; Sugar: 0.7g

Fat 74% / Protein 18% / Carbs 8%

Lemon Mint Grilled Prawns

Serves: 4 / Preparation time: 16 minutes / Cooking time: 12 minutes

2 lb. fresh prawn

2 tablespoons chopped mint leaves

¼ teaspoon thyme

2 tablespoons chopped parsley

4 teaspoons minced garlic

¼ cup extra virgin olive oil

2 tablespoons lemon juice

¼ cup carrot stick

¼ cup chopped lettuce

½ cup grated cheddar cheese

- Place mint leaves, thyme, chopped parsley, minced garlic, lemon juice, and extra virgin olive oil in a blender then blend until incorporated.
- Drizzle the spice mixture over the prawns then toss until the prawn is completely seasoned.
- Preheat a grill over medium heat then wait until it is ready.
- In the meantime, preheat a steamer and steam the carrot until tender. Set aside.
- Once the grill is ready, place the prawns on it. Grill for a few minutes until the prawns are completely cooked and brush with the spices once in a while.
- When the prawn is done, remove from grill and place on a serving dish.
- Garnish with lettuce and steamed carrots then sprinkle grated cheddar cheese on top.
- Serve and enjoy.

Per Serving: Net Carbs: 1.4g; Calories: 238; Total Fat: 19.6g; Saturated Fat: 5.6g
Protein: 14.3g; Carbs: 1.8g; Fiber: 0.4g; Sugar: 0.3g

Fat 74% / Protein 14% / Carbs 2%

Tuna Garlic Salad with Jalapeno Coleslaw

Serves: 4 / Preparation time: 14 minutes / Cooking time: 14 minutes

½ lb. tuna fillet

2 tablespoons lemon juice

2 tablespoons minced garlic

A pinch of black pepper

2 tablespoons butter

1 fresh apple

1 medium carrot

2 cups shredded cabbage

1 green jalapeno

3 tablespoons mayonnaise

1 ½ tablespoons extra virgin olive oil

- Drizzle lemon juice over the tuna fillet then let it rest for approximately 10 minutes.
- In the meantime, cut the apple into small pieces then place in a bowl.
- Quickly peel the carrot and shred it into pieces.
- Next, cup the green jalapeno into slices then combine with apple dices, shredded carrots, shredded cabbage.
- Drizzle extra virgin olive oil over the coleslaw then toss to combine. Set aside.
- After 10 minutes, rub the tuna fillet with minced garlic and pepper then set aside.
- In the meantime, preheat a grill over medium heat then wait until it reaches the desired temperature.
- Once the grill is ready, brush the tuna fillet with butter then place directly on the grill.
- Grill the tuna for approximately 5 minutes each side or until the tuna fillet is cooked through.
- Remove the tuna from the grill then serve with jalapeno coleslaw and mayonnaise.

Per Serving: Net Carbs: 5.9g; Calories: 352; Total Fat: 30.2g; Saturated Fat: 3g
Protein: 14.2g; Carbs: 7.3g; Fiber: 1.4g; Sugar: 2.6g

Fat 77% / Protein 16% / Carbs 7%

Calamari Mayo with Cauliflower Broccoli Salad

Serves: 4 / Preparation time: 16 minutes / Cooking time: 13 minutes

¾ lb. fresh squids

1 egg

¼ teaspoon pepper

1 cup almond flour

½ cup extra virgin olive oil, to fry

1-cup broccoli florets

1-cup cauliflower florets

¼ cup diced cheddar cheese

2 tablespoons diced onion

¼ cup mayonnaise

¼ cup sour cream

1-tablespoon lemon juice

- Preheat a steamer over medium heat then steam broccoli and cauliflower florets until tender. Set aside.
- Remove the squid ink and cut the squids into rings.
- Crack the egg then place in a bowl.
- Season the egg with pepper and stir until incorporated.
- Dip the squids in the beaten egg then roll in the almond flour. Set aside.
- Preheat a frying pan over medium heat then pour extra virgin olive oil into it.
- Once the oil is hot, put the rolled squids into the frying pan and fry for a few minutes or until lightly golden brown.
- Remove the squids from the frying pan and discard the excessive oil.
- Next, combine mayonnaise with sour cream and lemon juice then mix well.
- To serve, place the fried calamari on a serving dish then arrange the steamed broccoli and cauliflower florets on the same serving dish.
- Drizzle mayonnaise mixture over the salad then sprinkle diced cheddar cheese on to.
- Serve and enjoy immediately.

Per Serving: Net Carbs: 6g; Calories: 452; Total Fat: 39.3g; Saturated Fat: 7.5g
Protein: 19.3g; Carbs: 8.2g; Fiber: 2g; Sugar: 2g

Fat 78% / Protein 17% / Carbs 5%

Fried Crab Garlic with Zucchini Pickles

Serves: 4 / Preparation time: 11 minutes / Cooking time: 26 minutes

4 soft shell crabs

4 tablespoons minced garlic

½ cup extra virgin olive oil

1 medium zucchini

½ cup chopped onion

2 teaspoons celery seeds

1-teaspoon turmeric

1-cup apple cider vinegar

- Cut the zucchini into thin slices then place in a jar with a lid.
- Add chopped onion, celery seeds, and turmeric to the jar then pour apple cider vinegar to the jar.
- Cover the jar with the lid and shake for a few seconds. Store the pickles in the refrigerator.
- Place the crabs in the pot then pour water to cover.
- Season with minced garlic then bring to boil.
- Once it is boiled, turn the stove off and cover the pot with the lid. Let it rest for approximately 5 minutes.
- After 5 minutes, open the pot and take the crabs out of the pot.
- Preheat a frying pan over medium heat then pour extra virgin olive oil into it.
- Once it is hot, put the crabs into the frying pan then fry until crispy.
- Once it is done, remove from the frying pan and transfer to a serving dish.
- Serve with zucchini pickles.

Per Serving: Net Carbs: 5.8g; Calories: 385; Total Fat: 29.4g; Saturated Fat: 4.1g
Protein: 21.5g; Carbs: 7.1g; Fiber: 1.3g; Sugar: 1.8g

Fat 70% / Protein 24% / Carbs 6%

Spinach Salmon Nugget

Serves: 4 / Preparation time: 11 minutes / Cooking time: 21 minutes

½ lb. salmon fillet

½ teaspoon pepper

3 teaspoons minced garlic

1 egg

1 cup chopped spinach

½ cup extra virgin olive oil, to fry

- Preheat a steamer over medium heat then steam the spinach for a few minutes or until just wilted. Remove from the steamer.
- Cut the salmon fillet into cubes then place in a food processor then add minced garlic and pepper to the food processor. Process until smooth.
- Crack the egg and add to the salmon mixture.
- Add chopped steamed spinach to the mixture then mix until just combined.
- Preheat a steamer again then prepare a baking pan. Line the baking pan with aluminum foil.
- Place the salmon mixture in the steamer then steam for approximately 10 minutes or until set.
- Once it is done, remove from the steamer and let it cool for a few minutes.
- Take the salmon nugget out of the baking pan and cut into thick slices.
- Next, preheat a frying pan and pour extra virgin olive oil into it.
- Put the sliced salmon nugget in the frying pan and fry until both sides are lightly golden brown.
- Take the fried salmon nugget out of the frying pan and strain the excessive oil.
- Arrange the fried salmon nuggets on a serving dish and serve.
- Enjoy warm.

Per Serving: Net Carbs: 2.7g; Calories: 445; Total Fat: 37.8g; Saturated Fat: 6g
Protein: 25.2g; Carbs: 5.6g; Fiber: 2.9g; Sugar: 0.6g

Fat 76% / Protein 22% / Carbs 2%

Savory Fried Prawn with Red Chili Sauce and Steamed Collard Green

Serves: 4 / Preparation time: 9 minutes / Cooking time: 11 minutes

½ lb. fresh prawns

3 tablespoons minced garlic

2 teaspoons coriander

½ cup extra virgin olive oil, to fry

3 shallots

¼ cup red chili

1 medium red tomatoes

2 cups collard green

- Season the prawn with minced garlic and coriander then let it rest for approximately 10 minutes.

- In the meantime, preheat a steamer over medium heat then steam the collard green until tender. Remove from the steamer and set aside.

- Preheat a frying pan over medium heat then pour extra virgin olive oil into it.

- Once the oil is hot, put the prawns in the frying pan and fry for a few minutes or until the prawns turn into pink.

- Remove the fried prawns from the frying pan and place on a serving dish.

- Stir in red chili, shallots, and red tomatoes to the frying pan then fry for a few minutes or until wilted.

- Transfer the fried chili, shallots, and tomatoes to a food processor then process until smooth.

- To serve, place the steamed collard green and red chili sauce next to the fried prawn and enjoy warm.

Per Serving: Net Carbs: 4.6g; Calories: 353; Total Fat: 28.3g; Saturated Fat: 4g
Protein: 21g; Carbs: 5.8g; Fiber: 1.2g; Sugar: 0.8g

Fat 72% / Protein 23% / Carbs 5%

Tuna Cheese Steak with Asparagus Lemon Salad

Serves: 4 / Preparation time: 12 minutes / Cooking time: 19 minutes

1 lb. tuna fillet

3 tablespoons extra virgin olive oil

½ teaspoon pepper

½ handful asparagus

2 tablespoons lemon juice

½ teaspoon grated lemon zest

¼ cup mayonnaise

½ cup grated cheddar cheese

- Preheat a saucepan over medium heat then pour olive oil into it.
- Sprinkle pepper over the tuna and once the oil is hot, place the tuna in the saucepan.
- Cook the tuna for approximately 4 minutes or until opaque then flip it.
- Continue cooking the tuna for another 4 minutes or until the tuna is lightly golden brown and cooked through.
- Remove the tuna from the saucepan then place on a serving dish.
- Next, cut and trim the asparagus then sauté with the remaining olive oil.
- Once it is done, place the asparagus next to the tuna then set aside.
- Quickly combine mayonnaise with lemon juice and grated lemon zest then stir well.
- Drizzle the lemon mayonnaise over the tuna and asparagus then sprinkle grated cheese on top.
- Serve and enjoy.

Per Serving: Net Carbs: 0.7g; Calories: 656; Total Fat: 59.7g; Saturated Fat: 5.4g
Protein: 29.9g; Carbs: 0.9g; Fiber: 0.2g; Sugar: 0.5g

Fat 82% / Protein 17% / Carbs 1%

Stir Fry Crab in Creamy Chili

Serves: 4 / Preparation time: 11 minutes / Cooking time: 21 minutes

4 whole crabs

4 tablespoons minced garlic

¼ cup extra virgin olive oil

½ cup chopped onion

2 teaspoons chopped green chili

¾ cup coconut milk

2 kaffir lime leaves

1-cup fresh basil

2 tablespoons lemon juice

- Cut the crabs into halves then set aside.
- Preheat a skillet over medium heat then pour extra virgin olive oil into the skillet.
- Once the oil is hot, stir in minced garlic then sauté until wilted and aromatic.
- Add halved crabs to the skillet then stir until cooked and crispy.
- Remove the crabs from heat then place on a plate.
- Stir in chopped onion and green chili to the skillet then sauté with the remaining olive oil.
- Pour coconut milk over the onion then season with kaffir lime leaves. Bring to a simmer.
- Add fresh basils to the skillet then return the crabs to the skillet. Cook for approximately 2 minutes.
- Once it is done, remove from heat then drizzle lemon juice over the crabs.
- Transfer the crabs to a serving dish then enjoy.

Per Serving: Net Carbs: 7g; Calories: 320; Total Fat: 25.9g; Saturated Fat: 12.6g
Protein: 2g; Carbs: 8.6g; Fiber: 1.6g; Sugar: 3.3g

Fat 73% / Protein 18% / Carbs 9%

Yellow Squid Curry with Chopped Cabbage

Serves: 4 / Preparation time: 9 minutes / Cooking time: 12 minutes

1 lb. fresh squids

2 tablespoons extra virgin olive oil

2 teaspoons minced garlic

2 teaspoons sliced shallots

½ teaspoon turmeric

1-teaspoon curry powder

1 bay leaf

1 lemon grass

1-inch galangal

1 kaffir lime leaf

1-cup coconut milk

½ cup chopped cabbage

- Discard the squid ink then wash and rinse the squids.
- Preheat a skillet over medium heat then pour extra virgin olive oil into it.
- Once the oil is hot, stir in minced garlic and sliced shallots then sauté until aromatic and wilted.
- Stir in the squids then season with turmeric, curry powder, bay leaf, lemon grass, galangal, and kaffir lime leaf then sauté until wilted and completely seasoned.
- Pour coconut milk over the squids then bring to boil.
- Once it is boiled, remove from heat and transfer to a serving dish.
- Serve and enjoy.

Per Serving: Net Carbs: 6.9g; Calories: 288; Total Fat: 22.6g; Saturated Fat: 14g
Protein: 14.9g; Carbs: 8.6g; Fiber: 1.7g; Sugar: 2.1g

Fat 71% / Protein 19% / Carbs 10%

Baked Juicy Salmon with Sautéed Leek and Asparagus

Serves: 4 / Preparation time: 11 minutes / Cooking time: 26 minutes

1 lb. salmon fillet

6 tablespoons extra virgin olive

2 tablespoons lemon juice

2 teaspoons minced garlic

½ cup chopped leek

½ cup chopped asparagus

½ teaspoon pepper

½ teaspoon ginger

- Preheat an oven to 400°F (204°C) and prepare a baking tray. Set aside.
- Drizzle lemon juice over the salmon fillet then brush with extra virgin olive oil.
- Wrap the salmon fillet with aluminum foil then place on the baking tray.
- Place the baking tray in the oven and bake for approximately 10 minutes.
- After 10 minutes, take the baking tray out of the oven and unwrap the aluminum foil.
- Return the salmon back to the oven and bake again for another 10 minutes or until the salmon is lightly golden brown.
- In the meantime, preheat a saucepan over medium heat and pour olive oil into the saucepan.
- Once the oil is hot, stir in minced garlic then sauté until lightly golden brown.
- Next, add chopped leek and asparagus to the saucepan then season with pepper and ginger. Stir occasionally and cook until the vegetables are wilted.
- Transfer the sautéed vegetables to a serving dish then wait until the baked salmon is ready.
- When the salmon is done, take it out of the oven and place on the top of the vegetables.
- Serve and enjoy!

Per Serving: Net Carbs: 2.5g; Calories: 413; Total Fat: 32.4g; Saturated Fat: 5g
Protein: 27.7g; Carbs: 3.2g; Fiber: 0.7g; Sugar: 0.9g

Fat 71% / Protein 27% / Carbs 2%

Crispy Prawn with Almond Cheesy Sauce

Serves: 4 / Preparation time: 11 minutes / Cooking time: 16 minutes

½ lb. fresh prawns

1 egg

½ teaspoon pepper

1 cup almond flour

¼ cup extra virgin olive oil, to fry

¼ cup chopped onion

¼ cup water

½ cup grated cheese

- Peel the prawns and remove the head.
- Crack the egg then place in a bowl.
- Season the egg with pepper then stir until incorporated.
- Dip the prawns in the egg then roll into the almond flour. Set aside.
- Preheat a frying pan over medium heat then pour extra virgin olive oil into it.
- Once the oil is hot, put the prawns in the frying pan and fry until the prawns are lightly golden brown.
- Remove the fried prawns from the frying pan and strain the excessive oil. Arrange on a serving dish.
- Take about 2 tablespoons of extra virgin olive oil then pour into a saucepan. Preheat it over medium heat.
- When the oil is hot, stir in chopped onion and sauté until wilted and aromatic.
- Pour water into the saucepan then add grated cheese to the saucepan. Bring to a simmer.
- Stir in 1 tablespoon of almond flour and stir until thick.
- Drizzle the cheese sauce over the fried prawns then serve.
- Enjoy!

Per Serving: Net Carbs: 2.4g; Calories: 291; Total Fat: 22.8g; Saturated Fat: 5.7g
Protein: 19.4g; Carbs: 3.3g; Fiber: 0.9g; Sugar: 0.7g

Fat 71% / Protein 26% / Carbs 3%

Oyster Stew Creamy Kale

Serves: 4 / Preparation time: 9 minutes / Cooking time: 19 minutes

1 lb. oyster

2 tablespoons extra virgin olive oil

2 teaspoons sliced shallots

2 tablespoons chopped celeries

1-cup coconut milk

1-teaspoon thyme

½ teaspoon pepper

2 cups chopped kale

- Place the oyster in a pot then pour water to cover. Bring to boil.
- Once it is boiled, reduce the heat and cook for approximately 10 minutes.
- Strain the oysters then discard the water. Set aside.
- Next, preheat a skillet over medium heat then pour extra virgin olive oil into the skillet.
- Stir in sliced shallots and sauté until wilted and aromatic.
- Pour coconut milk into the skillet then bring to boil.
- Once it is boiled, season with thyme and pepper then stir in chopped kale. Bring to a simmer.
- Transfer to a serving dish then serve.
- Enjoy!

Per Serving: Net Carbs: 5.2g; Calories: 207; Total Fat: 18.9g; Saturated Fat: 10.8g
Protein: 19.4g; Carbs: 6.7g; Fiber: 1.5g; Sugar: 1.9g

Fat 82% / Protein 8% / Carbs 10%

Tuna Balls in Garlic Tomato Gravy

Serves: 4 / Preparation time: 14 minutes / Cooking time: 23 minutes

¾ lb. tuna fillet

1-tablespoon coconut flour

2 tablespoons chopped leek

2 tablespoons extra virgin olive oil

3 teaspoons minced garlic

4 cups water

½ teaspoon pepper

½ cup chopped tomato

¼ cup chopped celeries

- Cut the tuna fillet into cubes then place in a food processor.
- Add coconut flour into the food processor then process until smooth.
- Transfer the tuna mixture to a bowl then add chopped leek to the bowl. Mix until just combined.
- Shape the tuna mixture into small balls form then set aside.
- Pour2 cups of water into a pot then bring to boil.
- Once the water is boiled, slowly put the small tuna balls then cook until they are floating.
- In the meantime, preheat a skillet over medium heat then pour extra virgin olive oil into the skillet.
- Once the oil is hot, stir in minced garlic then sauté until aromatic.
- Pour the remaining water into the skillet then bring to boil.
- Once it is boiled, season the gravy with pepper then add chopped tomatoes and celeries to the gravy.
- When the tuna balls are floating, take them out of the pot and transfer to the gravy. Bring to a simmer.
- Transfer to a serving bowl then serve warm.
- Enjoy immediately.

Per Serving: Net Carbs: 2.5g; Calories: 449; Total Fat: 38.6g; Saturated Fat: 1.5g
Protein: 21.9g; Carbs: 4.3g; Fiber: 1.8g; Sugar: 1.1g

Fat 77% / Protein 21% / Carbs 2%

Tasty Asparagus Crab Soup

Serves: 4 / Preparation time: 7 minutes / Cooking time: 22 minutes

½ lb. crabmeat

½ lb. chopped asparagus

2 tablespoons extra virgin olive oil

½ cup chopped onion

2 teaspoons minced garlic

½ cup cauliflower florets

2 cups water

2 tablespoons chopped parsley

½ teaspoon pepper

2 eggs

- Preheat a skillet over medium heat then pour extra virgin olive oil into the skillet.
- Once the oil is hot, stir in chopped onion and minced garlic then sauté until wilted and aromatic.
- Pour water into the skillet over the spice and bring to boil.
- Once it is boiled, season the soup with pepper then stir in crabmeat, asparagus, and cauliflower florets.
- Cook the soup for approximately 10 minutes or until the asparagus is tender.
- Crack the eggs over boiled gravy and quickly stir well.
- Transfer the soup to a serving bowl then garnish with chopped parsley.
- Serve and enjoy.

Per Serving: Net Carbs: 2.5g; Calories: 118; Total Fat: 9.5g; Saturated Fat: 1.7g
Protein: 5.3g; Carbs: 3.5g; Fiber: 1g; Sugar: 1.3g

Fat 72% / Protein 20% / Carbs 8%

Green Chili Squid Black Pepper

Serves: 4 / Preparation time: 4 minutes / Cooking time: 16 minutes

½ lb. fresh squids

3 tablespoons extra virgin olive oil

2 teaspoons minced garlic

2 teaspoons sliced shallots

¼ cup chopped green chili

½ cup coconut milk

1-teaspoon coconut aminos

1-teaspoon black pepper

- Remove the squid ink and cut the squids into rings.
- Preheat a skillet over medium heat then pour extra virgin olive oil into the skillet.
- Once the oil is hot, stir in minced garlic and sliced shallots then sauté until wilted and aromatic.
- Next, add the squid to the skillet and sauté until just wilted.
- Pour coconut milk over the squids then cook until the liquid is completely absorbed into the squids.
- Add chopped green chili, coconut aminos, and black pepper to the skillet then stir until the squids are completely seasoned and cooked through.
- Remove the squids from heat and transfer to a serving dish.
- Serve and enjoy.

Per Serving: Net Carbs: 5.4g; Calories: 235; Total Fat: 18.7g; Saturated Fat: 8.1g
Protein: 11.9g; Carbs: 6.2g; Fiber: 0.8g; Sugar: 1.1g

Fat 72% / Protein 19% / Carbs 9%

Healthy Pan Seared Salmon with Mushroom and Spinach

Serves: 4 / Preparation time: 4 minutes / Cooking time: 16 minutes

1 lb. salmon fillet

3 tablespoons extra virgin olive oil

1 cup chopped mushroom

2 cups chopped spinach

¼ cup chopped tomatoes

½ teaspoon pepper

1-tablespoon balsamic vinegar

- Sprinkle pepper over the salmon fillet then set aside.
- Preheat a pan over medium heat then pour olive oil into it.
- Once it is hot, put the salmon in the pan and sear it for approximately 4 minutes then flip it.
- Sear the other side of the salmon and cook until it is completely done and both sides of the salmon are lightly golden brown.
- Remove the cooked salmon from the pan and transfer to a plate.
- Next, stir in mushroom then sauté with the remaining olive oil.
- Once the mushroom is wilted, stir in chopped spinach and tomatoes then toss with balsamic vinegar.
- Transfer the vegetables to a serving dish then put the cooked salmon on top.
- Serve and enjoy.

Per Serving: Net Carbs: 0.9g; Calories: 275; Total Fat: 21.6g; Saturated Fat: 3.3g
Protein: 19.1g; Carbs: 1.6g; Fiber: 0.7g; Sugar: 0.7g

Fat 71% / Protein 27% / Carbs 2%

Steamed Prawns with Green Basils and Light Spinach Soup

Serves: 4 / Preparation time: 6 minutes / Cooking time: 14 minutes

1 lb. fresh prawns

2 teaspoons minced garlic

¼ cup red chili flakes

½ cup chopped tomatoes

2 lemongrasses

1-cup fresh basils

½ cup grated coconut

1-cup coconut milk

2 cups chopped spinach

2 teaspoons sliced shallots

1-½ cups water

- Season the coconut milk with red chili flakes and minced garlic then stir well. Set aside.
- Preheat a steamer over medium heat then prepare a disposable aluminum pan.
- Combine the prawn with chopped tomatoes, lemon grasses, fresh basils, and grated coconut then stir well.
- Place the mixture in the prepared aluminum pan then spread evenly.
- Pour the coconut milk over the mixture then steam for approximately 15 minutes.
- In the meantime, pour water into a pot then bring to boil.
- Once it is boiled, stir in chopped spinach and season with sliced shallots. Stir well and remove from heat.
- When the steamed prawn is done, remove from the steamer and transfer to a serving dish.
- Serve with spinach soup.
- Enjoy.

Per Serving: Net Carbs: 3.3g; Calories: 231; Total Fat: 17.8g; Saturated Fat: 15.7g
Protein: 12.6g; Carbs: 7.7g; Fiber: 3g; Sugar: 3.6g

Fat 70% / Protein 24% / Carbs 6%

Mixed Tuna Soup in Green Coconut Gravy

Serves: 4 / Preparation time: 4 minutes / Cooking time: 16 minutes

½ lb. tuna fillet

2 tablespoons extra virgin olive oil

2 teaspoons sliced garlic

2 teaspoons sliced shallots

2 teaspoons green chili

½ cup fresh basil

1 bay leaf

1-inch galangal

1-cup coconut milk

1-cup water

½ cup chopped eggplant

½ cup chopped kale

½ cup chopped spinach

- Place garlic, shallots, and green chili in the food processor then process until smooth.
- Preheat a skillet over medium heat then pour extra virgin olive into it.
- Once it is hot, stir in the spice mixture then sauté until aromatic.
- Pour water over the spice then bring to boil.
- Once it is boiled, add tuna, eggplant, kale, and spinach then season with fresh basil, bay leaf, and galangal.
- Pour coconut milk into the skillet then bring to boil.
- Once it is boiled, remove the soup from heat and transfer to a serving dish.
- Serve and enjoy warm.

Per Serving: Net Carbs: 2.4g; Calories: 302; Total Fat: 26.5g; Saturated Fat: 1.1g
Protein: 13.9g; Carbs: 3.1g; Fiber: 0.7g; Sugar: 0.5g

Fat 79% / Protein 18% / Carbs 3%

Fish Balls with Chives and Lemon Garlic Creamy Sauce

Serves: 4 / Preparation time: 6 minutes / Cooking time: 24 minutes

½ lb. fish fillet

4 tablespoons extra virgin olive oil

½ cup chopped onion

4 teaspoons minced garlic

½ cup chives

1 egg

2-tablespoon coconut flour

2 tablespoons lemon juice

1 ½ cups coconut milk

- Preheat a skillet over medium heat then pour 2 tablespoons of extra virgin olive oil into it.
- Once it is hot, stir in chopped onion and sauté until wilted and aromatic. Remove from heat.
- Preheat an oven to 350°F (177°C) and line a baking tray with aluminum foil. Set aside.
- Cut the fish fillet into cubes then place in a food processor.
- Add sautéed onion, ¼ cup chives, egg, and a tablespoon of coconut flour to the food processor then process until smooth.
- Shape the mixture into small balls form then arrange on the prepared baking tray.
- Place the baking tray in the oven and bake the fish balls for approximately 20 minutes or until the fish balls are set.
- In the meantime, preheat a saucepan over medium heat then pour the remaining extra virgin olive oil into it.
- Once it is hot, stir in minced garlic to the saucepan and sauté until wilted and aromatic.
- Combine the remaining coconut flour into coconut milk then stir until incorporated.
- Pour into the saucepan then bring to a simmer.
- Once it is done, remove from heat and drizzle lemon juice on top. Stir well.
- When the fish balls are done, remove from the oven and transfer to a serving dish.
- Drizzle the sauce over the fish balls then serve.
- Enjoy warm.

Per Serving: Net Carbs: 6.8g; Calories: 476; Total Fat: 37.7g; Saturated Fat: 22.4g
Protein: 25g; Carbs: 11.8g; Fiber: 5g; Sugar: 4.5g

Fat 71% / Protein 23% / Carbs 6%

Spicy Crispy Squids with Onion

Serves: 4 / Preparation time: 4 minutes / Cooking time: 14 minutes

½ lb. fresh squids

1 big onion

1-cup almond flour

½ teaspoon pepper

1 egg

¾ cup water

½ cup extra virgin olive oil, to fry

¼ cup chopped red chili

2 teaspoons minced garlic

- Cut the squids and onion into rings then set aside.
- Place almond flour in a bowl then season with pepper.
- Crack the egg and add to the almond flour then pour water over the almond flour. Stir until incorporated. Set aside.
- Preheat a frying pan over medium heat then pour olive oil into it.
- Dip the onion ring in the almond flour mixture then fry.
- Once the onion is done, do the same thing to the squids.
- Next, take about 2 tablespoons of olive oil then pour into a pan.
- Stir in minced garlic and chopped red chili then sauté until wilted and aromatic.
- Add fried onion and squid rings to the pan then stir until the rings are completely seasoned.
- Remove from heat and transfer then crispy squids to a serving dish.
- Serve and enjoy warm.

Per Serving: Net Carbs: 6.5g; Calories: 358; Total Fat: 30.9g; Saturated Fat: 4.5g
Protein: 14.6g; Carbs: 8.6g; Fiber: 2.1g; Sugar: 2.6g

Fat 78% / Protein 15% / Carbs 7%

Salmon Lemon Black Pepper with Roasted Kale Garlic

Serves: 4 / Preparation time: 6 minutes / Cooking time: 41 minutes

¾ lb. salmon fillet

6 tablespoons extra virgin olive

1-teaspoon black pepper

2 fresh lemons

3 cups chopped kale

3 teaspoons minced garlic

- Preheat an oven to 400°F (204°C) and prepare 2 disposable aluminum pans.
- Cut the lemons into thin slices then arrange a half of the salmon slices on the bottom of the prepared aluminum pan.
- Brush the salmon fillet with olive oil then place on the lemon slices in the aluminum pan.
- Sprinkle black pepper over the salmon then cover the salmon with the remaining lemon slices.
- Place the salmon in the oven and bake for approximately 30 minutes or until the salmon is opaque and cooked through.
- In the meantime, place the chopped kale in another aluminum pan then drizzle the remaining olive oil over the kale.
- Season the kale with minced garlic and toss to combine.
- Once the salmon is done, remove it from the oven and put kale in it.
- Roast the kale for approximately 7 minutes or until done.
- Remove the kale from the oven and transfer to a serving dish together with the salmon.
- Serve and enjoy.

Per Serving: Net Carbs: 5.7g; Calories: 479; Total Fat: 37.6g; Saturated Fat: 6g
Protein: 31.5g; Carbs: 7.2g; Fiber: 1.5g; Sugar: 0.8g

Fat 71% / Protein 24% / Carbs 5%

Steamed Prawn and Veggie Bags

Serves: 4 / Preparation time: 6 minutes / Cooking time: 41 minutes

2 lbs. fresh shrimps

¼ cup diced carrot

¼ cup chopped leek

½ cup diced onion

4 tablespoons extra virgin olive oil

¼ cup coconut milk

2 eggs

¼ cup grated cheddar cheese

1 cup almond flour

½ cup water

- Combine almond flour with water then add an egg into the mixture. Stir until mixture.
- Make several omelets with this mixture then set aside.
- Peel the prawns and remove the head.
- Place the prawns in the food processor then process until smooth. Set aside.
- Next, preheat a skillet over medium heat then pour 2 tablespoons of olive oil into it.
- Once it is hot, stir in chopped onion and sauté until lightly golden brown and aromatic.
- Add carrot and leek to the skillet then pour coconut milk over the veggies. Cook until the coconut milk is completely absorbed into the veggies.
- Place the smooth prawn, sautéed veggies, and the remaining eggs in a bowl then mix until combined.
- Place an omelet on a flat surface then drop a tablespoon of prawn mixture on it.
- Fold like an envelope then set aside. Repeat with the remaining omelets and prawn mixture.
- Next, preheat a saucepan over medium heat then pour the remaining olive oil into it.
- Once the oil is hot, slowly put the prawn envelopes in the saucepan and cook for approximately 2 minutes.
- Flip them and cook for another 2 minutes or until both sides are lightly golden brown.
- Remove from the saucepan and arrange on a serving dish.
- Serve and enjoy warm.

Per Serving: Net Carbs: 3.7g; Calories: 315; Total Fat: 26g; Saturated Fat: 7.8g
Protein: 16.8g; Carbs: 5.4g; Fiber: 1.7g; Sugar: 2.1g

Fat 74% / Protein 21% / Carbs 5%

Carrot and Leek in Spicy Tuna Fritter

Serves: 4 / Preparation time: 16 minutes / Cooking time: 6 minutes

1 lb. tuna fillet

2 teaspoons red chili flakes

2 teaspoons minced garlic

½ cup chopped leek

¼ cup grated carrots

2 eggs

½ cup extra virgin olive oil, to fry

- Cut the tuna fillet into cubes then place in a food processor.
- Add red chili flakes, minced garlic, and eggs then process until smooth.
- Add chopped leek and grated carrots to the mixture then mix until just combined.
- Shape the tuna mixture into small fritter forms then set aside.
- Next, preheat a frying pan over medium heat then pour olive oil into it.
- Once the oil is hot, put the tuna fritters into the frying pan and fry for approximately 3 minutes.
- Flip the tuna fritters then fry for another 3 minutes or until both sides of the tuna fritters are lightly golden brown.
- Remove the fried tuna fritters from the frying pan and strain the excessive oil.
- Arrange the fried tuna on a serving dish then serve.
- Enjoy warm.

Per Serving: Net Carbs: 2.6g; Calories: 351; Total Fat: 35.2g; Saturated Fat: 4.3g
Protein: 8.4g; Carbs: 3g; Fiber: 0.4g; Sugar: 1g

Fat 90% / Protein 7% / Carbs 3%

Baked Calamari with Avocado Lemon Salsa

Serves: 4 / Preparation time: 12 minutes / Cooking time: 11 minutes

1 lb. fresh squid

1 cup almond flour

1 egg

4 tablespoons extra virgin olive oil

1 ripe avocado

2 tablespoons mayonnaise

¼ teaspoon pepper

1-teaspoon tomato puree

1 teaspoon lemon juice

- Crack the egg then place in a bowl.
- Pour extra virgin olive oil into the bowl then mix until incorporated.
- Remove the squid ink and put the squid in the egg mixture. Soak for a few minutes.
- Preheat an oven to 400°F (204°C) and line a baking tray with aluminum foil.
- Once the oven is ready, take the squids out of the marinade and transfer to the almond flour.
- Shake the squids several times until the squids are completely coated with flour.
- Transfer the coated squids to the prepared baking tray and spread evenly.
- Bake the squids for approximately 10 minutes then flip all of the squids.
- Bake again for another 10 minutes or until the squids is crispy and lightly golden brown.
- Remove the squids from the oven and transfer to a serving dish.
- Cut the avocado into halves then discard the seed.
- Scoop out the avocado flesh and mash until smooth and creamy.
- Add mayonnaise, pepper, tomato puree, and lemon juice to the avocado then mix until combined.
- Serve the baked squids with avocado lemon salsa.
- Enjoy!

Per Serving: Net Carbs: 5.4g; Calories: 390; Total Fat: 30.7g; Saturated Fat: 5.2g
Protein: 21.5g; Carbs: 9.6g; Fiber: 4.2g; Sugar: 0.6g

Fat 71% / Protein 23% / Carbs 6%

Zucchini Salmon Clear Soup

Serves: 4 / Preparation time: 6 minutes / Cooking time: 11 minutes

1 lb. salmon fillet

3 tablespoons extra virgin olive oil

1-teaspoon minced garlic

3 cups water

½ teaspoon pepper

½ teaspoon basil

½ teaspoon oregano

½ teaspoon ginger

1 cup chopped zucchini

- Cut the salmon fillet into cubes then set aside.
- Preheat a skillet over medium heat then pour extra virgin olive oil into it.
- Once the oil is hot, put the salmon cubes into the skillet then fry for a few minutes or until the salmon is lightly golden brown.
- Remove the salmon from the skillet then set aside.
- Stir in minced garlic and sauté until aromatic.
- Next, pour water into the skillet then season with pepper, basil, oregano, and ginger. Bring to boil.
- Once it is boiled, add chopped zucchini and fried salmon to the gravy and cook for approximately 2 minutes.
- Transfer the soup to a serving bowl then serve warm.
- Enjoy immediately.

Per Serving: Net Carbs: 0.8g; Calories: 276 Total Fat: 21.6g; Saturated Fat: 3.5g
Protein: 20.3g; Carbs: 1.2 g; Fiber: 0.4g; Sugar: 0.3g

Fat 70% / Protein 29% / Carbs 1%

Green Spaghetti with Cheesy White Prawn Sauce

Serves: 4 / Preparation time: 4 minutes / Cooking time: 16 minutes

½ lb. fresh prawns

2 tablespoons extra virgin olive oil

¾ cup diced onion

1 cup almond milk

1 cup diced cheddar cheese

1 tablespoon almond flour

3 medium zucchinis

2 tablespoons lemon juice

¼ teaspoon pepper

- Peel the zucchinis then discard the seeds.
- Using a julienne peeler cut the zucchinis into noodles form then place in a bowl.
- Drizzle lemon juice and sprinkle pepper over the zucchinis noodles then set aside.
- Next, preheat a saucepan over medium heat then pour olive oil into it.
- Once it is hot, stir in diced onion and sauté until wilted and aromatic.
- Add prawn to the saucepan and cook for a few minutes or until the prawns turn to pink.
- Combine almond flour with almond milk then pour into the saucepan.
- Stir in cheddar cheese and cook for a few minutes or until the cheese is melted. Remove from heat.
- Drizzle the cheese prawn sauce over the zucchini noodles then mix well.
- Serve and enjoy immediately.

Per Serving: Net Carbs: 6.5g; Calories: 407; Total Fat: 31.9g; Saturated Fat: 20g
Protein: 22.5g; Carbs: 9.9g; Fiber: 3.4g; Sugar: 4.7g

Fat 71% / Protein 23% / Carbs 6%

Tomato Creamy Tuna with Sautéed Broccoli and Cauliflower

Serves: 4 / Preparation time: 3 minutes / Cooking time: 13 minutes

½ lb. tuna fillet

3 tablespoons extra virgin olive oil

½ cup chopped onion

1-cup tomato puree

½ teaspoon pepper

½ teaspoon oregano

1-cup broccoli florets

1-cup cauliflower florets

2 tablespoons almond butter

- Preheat a skillet over medium heat then pour olive oil into it.
- Once the oil is hot, put the tuna into the skillet and fry until the tuna is lightly golden brown.
- Remove the tuna from the skillet then set aside.
- Next, stir in chopped onion and sauté until lightly golden brown and aromatic.
- After that, pour tomato puree into the skillet and season with pepper and oregano.
- Bring to a simmer then add fried tuna to the skillet. Stir well and cook for approximately 2 minutes.
- In the meantime, preheat a saucepan over medium heat then add almond butter to the saucepan.
- Stir in broccoli florets and cauliflower florets to the saucepan then sauté until aromatic. Cook until the vegetables are tender but still crunchy.
- Once everything is done, transfer the tuna to a serving dish together with the gravy and serve with sautéed broccoli and cauliflower.
- Enjoy!

Per Serving: Net Carbs: 4.4g; Calories: 392 Total Fat: 34.5g; Saturated Fat: 1.9g
Protein: 16.5g; Carbs: 7g; Fiber: 2.6g; Sugar: 2g

Fat 79% / Protein 83% / Carbs 4%

Coconut Crab Cakes with Green Leaves

Serves: 4 / Preparation time: 11 minutes / Cooking time: 16 minutes

¼ lb. crabmeat

½ teaspoon pepper

3 teaspoons minced garlic

½ cup coconut flakes

2 eggs

1 cup chopped spinach

¼ cup chopped leek

½ cup extra virgin olive oil, to fry

- Combine crabmeat with coconut flakes, eggs, chopped spinach, and chopped leek then season with pepper and minced garlic. Mix well.
- Shape the mixture into medium fritter forms then set aside.
- Next, preheat a frying pan over medium heat then pour extra virgin olive oil into the frying pan.
- Once the oil is done, put the crab fritter into the frying pan and fry for approximately 3 minutes.
- Flip the fritters then fry for another 3 minutes or until set and both sides of the fritters are lightly golden brown.
- Remove from the frying pan and strain the excessive oil.
- Once it is done, arrange the crab cakes on a serving dish then enjoy with sautéed veggie, as you desired.

Per Serving: Net Carbs: 2.1g; Calories: 313; Total Fat: 31.3g; Saturated Fat: 7.2g
Protein: 6.9g; Carbs: 3.3g; Fiber: 1.2g; Sugar: 1g

Fat 90% / Protein 7% / Carbs 3%

Squid Tomato Soup with Oregano

Serves: 4 / Preparation time: 4 minutes / Cooking time: 22 minutes

¾ lb. fresh squid

2 tablespoons extra virgin olive oil

½ lb. red tomatoes

2 cups water

½ cup coconut milk

½ cup chopped onion

2 teaspoons minced garlic

1-tablespoon lemon juice

1-teaspoon oregano

2 cups chopped collard green

- Place the red tomatoes in a blender then pour water into it. Blend until smooth then set aside.
- Remove the squid ink then cut into rings. Set aside.
- Preheat a skillet over medium heat then pour extra virgin olive oil into the skillet.
- Once the oil is hot, stir in chopped onion and minced garlic then sauté until wilted and aromatic.
- Next, add squids to the skillet then sauté until just wilted.
- After that, pour the tomato mixture to the skillet then season with oregano. Bring to boil.
- Once it is boiled, stir in collard green and pour coconut milk into the skillet. Bring to a simmer.
- Once it is done, remove from heat and transfer to a serving bowl.
- Drizzle lemon juice over the soup then serve warm.
- Enjoy immediately.

Per Serving: Net Carbs: 7g; Calories: 283; Total Fat: 22.6g; Saturated Fat: 11.3g
Protein: 13.3g; Carbs: 9.8g; Fiber: 2.8g; Sugar: 3.5g

Fat 72% / Protein 18% / Carbs 10%

VEGETARIAN

Contents

Roasted Asparagus with Creamy Cashew Topping

Serves: 4 / Preparation time: 6 minutes / Cooking time: 14 minutes

½ lb. asparagus

2 tablespoons extra virgin olive oil

½ teaspoon black pepper

¼ cup butter

¼ cup roasted cashews

1-tablespoon sesame oil

¼ cup coconut milk

2 tablespoons lemon juice

2 teaspoons minced garlic

2 tablespoons coconut aminos

- Preheat an oven to 425°F (218°C) and line a baking tray with parchment paper. Set aside.
- Cut and trim the end of the asparagus then drizzle olive oil over the asparagus.
- Rub the asparagus with black pepper then spread over the prepared baking tray.
- Once the oven is ready, place the baking tray in the oven and bake the asparagus for approximately 15 minutes or until tender.
- In the meantime, place roasted cashew, butter, minced garlic, and coconut aminos in a food processor then pour sesame oil, coconut milk, and lemon juice over the cashews. Process until smooth then set aside.
- When the roasted asparagus is done, take it out of the oven and transfer to a serving dish.
- Drizzle cashew sauce over the roasted asparagus then serve warm.
- Enjoy!

Per Serving: Net Carbs: 6.3g; Calories: 300; Total Fat: 29.6g; Saturated Fat: 12.8g
Protein: 3.3g; Carbs: 8.3g; Fiber: 2g; Sugar: 2.2g

Fat 88% / Protein 4% / Carbs 8%

Super Simple Vegetables Salad

Serves: 4 / Preparation time: 4 minutes / Cooking time: 7 minutes

¾ cup chopped red tomatoes

1 cucumber

½ cup chopped green bell pepper

½ cup chopped onion

¼ cup pitted Kalamata olives

¼ cup extra virgin olive oil

2 tablespoons red vinegar

¼ cup mayonnaise

½ teaspoon oregano

- Cut the cucumber into thin slices then place in a salad bowl.
- Next, add chopped red tomatoes, chopped green bell pepper, chopped onion, and kalamata olives to the salad bowl then drizzle extra virgin olive oil and red vinegar over the vegetables. Toss to combine.
- Once it is done, transfer the salad to a serving dish then drizzle mayonnaise and sprinkle oregano on top.
- Serve and enjoy!

Per Serving: Net Carbs: 6.3g; Calories: 300; Total Fat: 29.6g; Saturated Fat: 12.8g
Protein: 3.3g; Carbs: 8.3g; Fiber: 2g; Sugar: 2.2g

Fat 91% / Protein 1% / Carbs 8%

Mushroom Black Pepper in Cabbage Blanket

Serves: 4 / Preparation time: 11 minutes / Cooking time: 22 minutes

2 cups mushroom

3 tablespoons extra virgin olive oil

1 teaspoon minced garlic

½ cup sliced onion

3 tablespoons coconut aminos

2 teaspoons cayenne pepper

¾ cup coconut milk

¼ teaspoon black pepper

¼ lb. cabbage

- Cut the mushroom s into small pieces then set aside.
- Preheat a skillet over medium heat then pour extra virgin olive oil into it.
- Once the olive oil is hot, stir in minced garlic and sliced onion to the skillet then sauté until aromatic and lightly golden brown.
- Next, add mushrooms to the skillet then season with black pepper.
- Pour coconut milk over the mushrooms then cook until the coconut milk is completely absorbed into the mushrooms.
- In the meantime, place the cabbage in the steamer then steam until wilted.
- Remove the steamed cabbage from the steamer and let it cool.
- Next, return back to the mushroom.
- Once the coconut milk is completely absorbed into the mushroom, season with cayenne pepper and coconut aminos then stir well. Remove from heat and let it cool.
- Place a sheet of steamed cabbage on a flat surface then put the cooked mushroom on it.
- Wrap the mushrooms with steamed cabbage and roll it tightly. Repeat with the remaining steamed cabbage and mushrooms.
- Serve and enjoy.

Per Serving: Net Carbs: 7.3g; Calories: 282; Total Fat: 27.3g; Saturated Fat: 11.9g
Protein: 3.2g; Carbs: 9.8g; Fiber: 2.5g; Sugar: 3.8g

Fat 73% / Protein 7% / Carbs 10%

Tasty Vegetables Soup in Coconut Gravy

Serves: 4 / Preparation time: 4 minutes / Cooking time: 11 minutes

2 cups chopped spinach

1 cup chopped cabbage

1 medium carrot

¼ cup cooked kidney beans

2 tablespoons chopped celeries

1 teaspoon minced garlic

1-teaspoon cayenne pepper

½ teaspoon red chili flakes

¾ cup coconut milk

1-cup water

- Peel the carrot then cut into slices. Set aside.
- Pour water into a pot then season with minced garlic, cayenne pepper, and red chili flakes then bring to boil.
- Once it is boiled, add kidney beans, chopped cabbage, and carrot to the soup.
- Pour coconut milk into the soup then bring to a simmer.
- Next, stir in chopped spinach to the soup and cook until the spinach is just wilted.
- Transfer the soup to a serving bowl then serve warm.
- Enjoy immediately.

Per Serving: Net Carbs: 5.2g; Calories: 137; Total Fat: 11g; Saturated Fat: 9.5g
Protein: 2.7g; Carbs: 9.6g; Fiber: 3.2g; Sugar: 4g

Fat 72% / Protein 18% / Carbs 10%

Avocado Cream Soup with Chipotle

Serves: 4 / Preparation time: 4 minutes / Cooking time: 12 minutes

4 ripe avocados

2 cups water

2 cups Greek yogurt

1-teaspoon chipotle

- Cut the avocados into halves then remove the seeds.
- Scoop out the avocado flesh then place in a blender.
- Pour Greek yogurt to the blender then blend until smooth. Set aside.
- Next, pour water into a saucepan then season with chipotle. Bring to boil.
- Once it is boiled, stir in avocado mixture then stir well.
- Transfer the avocado cream soup to a serving bowl then serve immediately.
- Enjoy warm.

Per Serving: Net Carbs: 6.5g; Calories: 477; Total Fat: 41.5g; Saturated Fat: 10.9g
Protein: 5.8g; Carbs: 20g; Fiber: 13.5g; Sugar: 3.8g

Fat 78% / Protein 17% / Carbs 5%

5 Minutes Crispy Spinach

Serves: 4 / Preparation time: 4 minutes / Cooking time: 2 minutes

2 bunches spinach

½ cup almond flour

¼ teaspoon pepper

1-cup water

½ cup extra virgin olive oil, to fry

- Season the almond flour with pepper then stir well. Set aside.
- Cut the spinach leaves and remove the stem.
- Coat the spinach leaves with almond flour mixture then dip into the water.
- Take the spinach out of the water then coat again with almond flour. Repeat with the remaining spinach and almond flour.
- Preheat a frying pan over medium heat then pour olive oil into it.
- Once the oil is hot, put the coated spinach in the hot oil and fry for approximately 2 minutes each side.
- Remove the fried spinach from the frying pan and strain the oil.
- Serve and enjoy.

Per Serving: Net Carbs: 2.8g; Calories: 299; Total Fat: 30.4g; Saturated Fat: 4.2g
Protein: 5.6g; Carbs: 7g; Fiber: 4.2g; Sugar: 0.8g

Fat 92% / Protein 7% / Carbs 1%

Sautéed Broccoli with Onion and Mushroom

Serves: 4 / Preparation time: 8 minutes / Cooking time: 6 minutes

3 cups broccoli florets

1 cup chopped mushroom

2 tablespoons extra virgin olive oil

½ cup chopped onion

¼ teaspoon pepper

½ teaspoon sesame seeds

- Preheat a skillet over medium heat then pour extra virgin olive oil into it.
- Once the oil is hot, stir in chopped onion and sauté until aromatic and lightly golden brown.
- Next, stir in chopped mushroom and broccoli florets then cook until wilted.
- Season the mushroom and broccoli with pepper then stir well. Cook until the broccoli is done but not too soft.
- Remove the sautéed broccoli and mushroom from heat and transfer to a serving dish.
- Sprinkle sesame seeds on top and serve immediately.
- Enjoy warm.

Per Serving: Net Carbs: 4.3g; Calories: 95; Total Fat: 7.5g; Saturated Fat: 1g
Protein: 2.7g; Carbs: 6.6g; Fiber: 2.3g; Sugar: 2.1g

Fat 71% / Protein 14% / Carbs 15%

Almond Pecan Porridge with Cinnamon

Serves: 4 / Preparation time: 4 minutes / Cooking time: 16 minutes

2 cups unsweetened almond milk

½ cup almond butter

2 tablespoons extra virgin olive oil

2 tablespoons hemp seeds

½ cup chopped pecans

1-teaspoon cinnamon

- Preheat an oven to 250°F (121°C)) and line a baking tray with parchment paper.
- Toss the pecans with extra virgin olive then spread over the prepared baking tray.
- Bake the pecans until tender then remove from the oven. Let it cool.
- Once the toasted pecans are cool, transfer to a food processor then process until becoming crumbles. Set aside.
- Preheat almond milk over medium heat then add almond butter to it.
- Wait until the butter is melted then transfer the mixture to a serving bowl.
- Add pecans crumbles to the bowl then sprinkle hemp seeds and cinnamon on top.
- Serve and enjoy immediately.

Per Serving: Net Carbs: 4g; Calories: 200; Total Fat: 17.5g; Saturated Fat: 1.8g
Protein: 6.8g; Carbs: 5.9g; Fiber: 1.9g; Sugar: 0.7g

Fat 79% / Protein 13% / Carbs 8%

Green Veggie Salad with Brown Cashew Sauce

Serves: 4 / Preparation time: 5 minutes / Cooking time: 7 minutes

2 cups chopped spinach

½ cup chopped long beans

1 cup chopped cabbage

½ cup beans sprouts

¼ cup shredded carrots

2 tablespoons extra virgin olive oil

1-teaspoon minced garlic

¼ cup roasted cashews

½ cup coconut milk

2 teaspoons red chili flakes

2 tablespoons coconut aminos

- Preheat a steamer over medium heat then alternately steam the vegetables.
- Remove the steamed vegetables then arrange on a serving dish. Set aside.
- Place the roasted cashews in a blender then pour coconut milk into the blender. Blend until smooth then set aside.
- Preheat a skillet over medium heat then pour olive oil into it.
- Stir in minced garlic then sauté until lightly golden brown and aromatic.
- Pour cashews and coconut milk mixture into the skillet then season with red chili flakes. Bring to a simmer.
- Once it is done, pour the cashews sauce over the steamed vegetables then drizzle coconut aminos on top.
- Serve and enjoy immediately.

Per Serving: Net Carbs: 6.6g; Calories: 172; Total Fat: 15.2g; Saturated Fat: 7.5g
Protein: 2.8g; Carbs: 8.8g; Fiber: 2.2g; Sugar: 3.7g

Fat 80% / Protein 5% / Carbs 15%

Carrot Omelet with Avocado Topping

Serves: 4 / Preparation time: 6 minutes / Cooking time: 8 minutes

½ cup grated carrots

½ cup chopped spinach

3 tablespoons coconut flour

½ cup coconut milk

3 tablespoons extra virgin olive oil

2 ripe avocados

½ teaspoon cinnamon

- Cut the avocados into halves then remove the seeds.
- After that, scoop out the avocado flesh then mash until smooth. Set aside.
- Combine coconut flour with coconut milk then stir until incorporated and smooth.
- Add grated carrot and chopped spinach to the mixture then stir until combined.
- Next, preheat a pan over medium heat then pour extra virgin olive oil into the pan.
- Once the oil is hot, pour coconut mixture to the pan then fry until both sides are lightly golden and the omelets cooked trough.
- Place the carrots omelets on a serving dish then top with the avocado topping.
- Sprinkle cinnamon over the avocado then serve.
- Enjoy!

Per Serving: Net Carbs: 6.3g; Calories: 416; Total Fat: 38.8g; Saturated Fat: 13.5g
Protein: 4.3g; Carbs: 18g; Fiber: 11.7g; Sugar: 3g

Fat 84% / Protein 10% / Carbs 6%

Light Sour Soup with Kabocha

Serves: 4 / Preparation time: 8 minutes / Cooking time: 6 minutes

1 cup chopped Kabocha

½ cup chopped long beans

¼ cup chopped carrots

¾ cup chopped cabbage

½ cup pecans

1-tablespoon extra virgin olive oil

½ teaspoon minced garlic

1-teaspoon sliced shallot

1-teaspoon red chili flakes

¼ cup chopped green tomatoes

3 cups water

- Pour water into a pot then bring to boil.
- Once it is boiled, add pecans to the pot then cook the pecans until tender.
- Remove the pecans from the pot and strain the water. Set aside.
- Next, preheat a pot over medium heat then pour olive oil into the pot.
- Once the oil is hot, stir in minced garlic and sliced shallots then sauté until aromatic and lightly golden.
- Pour water into the pot then season with red chili flakes. Bring to boil.
- Once it is boiled, reduce the heat and add kabocha, long beans, carrots, cabbages, pecans, and chopped green tomatoes to the pot. Cook for approximately 3 minutes or until the vegetables are tender.
- Transfer the soup to a serving bowl then serve immediately.
- Enjoy warm.

Per Serving: Net Carbs: 5.4g; Calories: 104; Total Fat: 8.3g; Saturated Fat: 0.9g
Protein: 1.6g; Carbs: 7g; Fiber: 1.6g; Sugar: 2.7g

Fat 72% / Protein 8% / Carbs 20%

Spiced Coconut Carrot Fritter

Serves: 4 / Preparation time: 4 minutes / Cooking time: 12 minutes

½ cup coconut flour

2 tablespoons coconut milk

2 tablespoons water

2 tablespoons grated coconut

2 tablespoons shredded carrots

¼ teaspoon coriander

¼ cup olive oil, to fry

- Place coconut flour in a bowl then pour water and coconut milk over the flour.
- Season the flour with coriander then mix until incorporated.
- Add grated coconut and shredded carrots to the mixture then stir until just combined.
- Next, preheat a frying pan over medium heat then pour olive oil into it.
- Once the oil is hot, drop about 2 tablespoons of mixture and fry for approximately 2 minutes.
- Flip the fritter and fry until both sides of the fritter are lightly golden brown.
- Remove the fritter and strain the excessive oil. Repeat with the remaining mixture.
- Once it is done, arrange the fritters on a serving dish and serve.
- Enjoy warm.

Per Serving: Net Carbs: 1g; Calories: 143; Total Fat: 15.5g; Saturated Fat: 4.4g
Protein: 0.5g; Carbs: 2.1g; Fiber: 1.1g; Sugar: 0.7g

Fat 97% / Protein 1% / Carbs 2%

Savory Kale Garlic with Crispy Coconut Cubes

Serves: 4 / Preparation time: 6 minutes / Cooking time: 22 minutes

1-cup coconut flour

½ cup water

5 tablespoons minced garlic

1-teaspoon pepper

¼ cup extra virgin olive oil, to sauté and fry

3 cups chopped kale

2 tablespoons coconut aminos

1 teaspoon red chili flakes

- Preheat a steamer over medium heat and wait until it is ready.
- In the meantime, combine coconut flour with water, 2 tablespoons of minced garlic, and ½ teaspoon pepper. Mix well until becoming a soft dough.
- Wrap the dough with aluminum foil then place in the steamer. Steam for about 10 minutes or until set.
- Remove the cooked dough from the steamer and let it cool.
- Once the cooked coconut dough is cool, unwrap it and cut into cubes. Set aside.
- Preheat a frying pan over medium heat then pour olive oil into it.
- Once the oil is hot, put the coconut cubes in the frying pan and fry until lightly golden brown and crispy.
- Remove the crispy coconut cubes from the frying pan then strain the excessive oil. Set aside.
- Next, take 2 tablespoons of olive oil and pour into a skillet.
- Preheat the skillet to medium heat then stir in the remaining minced garlic into it. Sauté until aromatic and lightly golden brown.
- Add chopped kale to the skillet then season with pepper, red chili flakes, and coconut aminos. Stir well and cook until the kale is wilted.
- Once it is done, remove the sautéed kale from the skillet and transfer to a serving dish.
- Serve and enjoy.

Per Serving: Net Carbs: 6.2g; Calories: 152; Total Fat: 13.2g; Saturated Fat: 2.3g
Protein: 2g; Carbs: 8.3g; Fiber: 2.1g; Sugar: 0.9g

Fat 78% / Protein 6% / Carbs 16%

Scrumptious Zucchini Noodles with Avocado Pecans Sauce

Serves: 4 / Preparation time: 4 minutes / Cooking time: 14 minutes

4 medium zucchinis

2 tablespoons extra virgin olive oil

1 fresh avocado

1-cup fresh basil leaves

½ cup roasted pecans

2 teaspoons minced garlic

2 tablespoons lemon juice

¼ cup water

- Cut the avocado into halves then remove the seed.
- Scoop out the avocado flesh then place in a blender.
- Add fresh basil leaves and roasted pecans to the blender then season with minced garlic and lemon juice.
- Pour water into the blender then blend until smooth. Set aside.
- Peel the zucchinis then cut into halves lengthwise.
- Using a julienne peeler cut the zucchini into noodles form then set aside.
- Next, preheat a skillet over medium heat then pour olive oil into it.
- Once the oil is hot, stir in the zucchini noodles and mix well.
- Sauté the zucchini until wilted then remove from heat. Transfer to a salad bowl.
- Drizzle avocado pecans sauce over the zucchini noodles then toss to combine.
- Serve and enjoy.

Per Serving: Net Carbs: 6.2g; Calories: 249; Total Fat: 22.5g; Saturated Fat: 3.6g
Protein: 4.3g; Carbs: 12.6g; Fiber: 6.4g; Sugar: 4.1g

Fat 81% / Protein 9% / Carbs 10%

Healthy Veggie Rolls with Dill Sauce

Serves: 4 / Preparation time: 4 minutes / Cooking time: 12 minutes

4 fresh collard green leaves

1 cucumber

½ red bell pepper

¼ cup diced onion

1 tablespoon sliced olives

¼ cup cherry tomatoes

½ cup almond yogurt

¾ teaspoon garlic powder

½ teaspoon vinegar

2 tablespoons extra virgin olive oil

5 sprigs fresh dill

¼ teaspoon pepper

- Combine almond yogurt with garlic powder, vinegar, olive oil, fresh dill, and pepper in a blender then blend until smooth. Set aside.
- Peel the cucumber and remove the seeds.
- Using a julienne peeler cut the cucumber into noodle forms then set aside. Do the same thing with the bell pepper.
- Arrange collard green leaves on a flat surface then spread the almond yogurt mixture over the leaves.
- After that, arrange cucumber noodles and bell pepper noodles on the leaves then sprinkle diced onion, sliced olives, and cherry tomatoes on top.
- Carefully roll the leaves then cut into halves.
- Arrange the rolls on a serving dish then serve. Enjoy!

Per Serving: Net Carbs: 6.9g; Calories: 111; Total Fat: 8.6g; Saturated Fat: 1.1g
Protein: 1.9g; Carbs: 8.8g; Fiber: 1.9g; Sugar: 3.8g

Fat 70% / Protein 5% / Carbs 25%

Baked Spaghetti Squash with Spicy Almond Sauce

Serves: 4 / Preparation time: 6 minutes / Cooking time: 24 minutes

½ spaghetti squash

2 tablespoons sesame oil

¼ cup almond butter

2 tablespoons coconut aminos

1 ½ tablespoons extra virgin olive oil

¼ teaspoon garlic powder

1 teaspoon red chili flakes

2 tablespoons chopped roasted almonds

- Preheat an oven to 250°F (121°C) and cover a baking tray with aluminum foil.
- Brush the spaghetti squash with sesame oil then place on the prepared baking tray.
- Bake the spaghetti squash for approximately 15 minutes or until tender then remove from the oven and let it cool.
- Using a julienne peeler cut the spaghetti squash into noodle forms then place in a salad bowl. Set aside.
- Next, combine almond butter with coconut aminos, extra virgin olive oil, garlic powder, and red chili flakes then stir until incorporated.
- Drizzle the sauce over the baked spaghetti squash then sprinkle chopped roasted almonds on top.
- Serve and enjoy!

Per Serving: Net Carbs: 2.2g; Calories: 139; Total Fat: 14.2g; Saturated Fat: 1.9g
Protein: 1.2g; Carbs: 3g; Fiber: 0.8g; Sugar: 1.1g

Fat 92% / Protein 2% / Carbs 6%

Savory and Nutritious Fried Cauliflower Rice

Serves: 4 / Preparation time: 6 minutes / Cooking time: 23 minutes

3 cups cauliflower florets

2 tablespoons extra virgin olive oil

½ teaspoon minced garlic

½ teaspoon pepper

2 tablespoons coconut aminos

1 lemon grass

1 cup chopped mushroom

½ cup sliced cabbage

¼ cup shredded carrots

- Place the cauliflower florets in a steamer then steam until soft.
- Remove the steamed cauliflower florets from the steamer and transfer to a food processor. Process until smooth.
- Next, preheat a skillet over medium heat then pour extra virgin olive oil into the skillet.
- Once the oil is hot, stir in minced garlic and sauté until wilted and aromatic.
- Add chopped mushrooms, sliced cabbage, and shredded carrots to the skillet then sauté until wilted.
- After that, stir in cauliflower rice to the skillet then season with pepper, coconut aminos, and lemon grass. Cook until combined.
- Once it is done, transfer the fried cauliflower rice to a serving dish then serve warm.
- Enjoy immediately.

Per Serving: Net Carbs: 4.3g; Calories: 92; Total Fat: 7.2g; Saturated Fat: 1g
Protein: 2.3g; Carbs: 6.8g; Fiber: 2.5g; Sugar: 2.7g

Fat 70% / Protein 12% / Carbs 18%

Fresh Green in Red Curry Gravy

Serves: 4 / Preparation time: 4 minutes / Cooking time: 16 minutes

2 cups broccoli florets

1 cup chopped spinach

1 cup chopped kale

2 tablespoons chopped celeries

2 tablespoons extra virgin olive oil

¼ cup chopped onion

2 teaspoons minced garlic

1-teaspoon ginger

1-teaspoon red curry paste

¾ cup coconut milk

½ cup water

- Preheat a skillet over medium heat then pour extra virgin olive oil into it.
- Once the oil is hot, stir in chopped onion and minced garlic then sauté until lightly golden brown and aromatic.
- Next, pour water into the skillet then season with ginger and red curry paste. Bring to boil.
- Once it is boiled, stir in broccoli florets, chopped spinach, and chopped kale to the skillet then pour coconut milk over the vegetables. Bring to a simmer.
- Once it is done, remove the vegetable curry from heat and transfer to a serving bowl.
- Serve and enjoy warm.

Per Serving: Net Carbs: 6.4g; Calories: 201; Total Fat: 18.4g; Saturated Fat: 10.6g
Protein: 3.3g; Carbs: 9.3g; Fiber: 2.9g; Sugar: 2.7g

Fat 82% / Protein 5% / Carbs 13%

Coconut Creamy Pumpkin Porridge

Serves: 4 / Preparation time: 6 minutes / Cooking time: 14 minutes

3 cups chopped pumpkin

2 cups water

½ cup coconut milk

¼ cup extra virgin olive oil

¼ teaspoon pepper

½ teaspoon garlic

½ teaspoon thyme

2 tablespoons chopped parsley

2 tablespoons coconut flakes

¼ cup chopped roasted almonds

- Preheat an oven to 250°F (121°C) and line a baking tray with aluminum foil.
- Toss the pumpkin cubes with extra virgin olive oil then spread on the prepared baking tray.
- Bake the pumpkin until tender then remove from the oven. Set aside.
- Pour water into a pot then season with pepper, garlic, and thyme. Bring to boil.
- Once it is boiled, add baked pumpkin to the pot and pour coconut milk over the pumpkin. Bring to a simmer.
- Once it is done, remove the cooked pumpkin and the gravy from heat then transfer to a blender. Blend until smooth and becoming porridge.
- Pour the creamy pumpkin to a serving bowl then sprinkle coconut flakes and roasted almonds on top.
- Garnish with fresh parsley then serve immediately.
- Enjoy warm.

Per Serving: Net Carbs: 7.2g; Calories: 265; Total Fat: 25.9g; Saturated Fat: 9.4g
Protein: 3.3g; Carbs: 9.5g; Fiber: 2.3g; Sugar: 2.7g

Fat 88% / Protein 2% / Carbs 10%

Spicy Eggplant in Coconut Gravy

Serves: 4 / Preparation time: 4 minutes / Cooking time: 14 minutes

2 cups chopped eggplants

2 tablespoons extra virgin olive oil

2 cloves garlic

2 shallots

¼ cup red chili flakes

1-inch galangal

2 lemon grasses

2 bay leaves

1 kaffir lime leaf

1-cup coconut milk

- Place garlic, shallots, and red chili flakes in a food processor then process until smooth.
- Next, preheat a skillet over medium heat then pour olive oil into it.
- Once the oil is hot, stir in the spice mixture then sauté until aromatic.
- Add chopped eggplants to the skillet then season with galangal, lemon grasses, bay leaves, and kaffir lime leaves.
- Pour coconut milk over the eggplants then bring to a simmer.
- Once it is done, transfer the cooked eggplants together with the gravy to a serving dish.
- Serve and enjoy!

Per Serving: Net Carbs: 5.8 g; Calories: 221; Total Fat: 21.5g; Saturated Fat: 13.7g
Protein: 1.9g; Carbs: 8.4g; Fiber: 2.6 g; Sugar: 3.5g

Fat 88% / Protein 2% / Carbs 10%

DESSERT

Contents

Almond Cheesy Cookie Dough

Serves: 4 / Preparation time: 14 minutes / Cooking time: 4 minutes

1 cup almond flour

½ cup almond butter

1 tablespoon flax seed

2 tablespoons water

1-cup cheese cream

- Preheat an oven to 225°F (107°C) and line a baking tray with parchment paper.
- Spread almond flour over the baking tray then toast for a few minutes until just lightly golden.
- In the meantime, combine flax seeds with 2 tablespoons of water then stir well. Set aside.
- Once the almond flour is done, remove from the oven and let it cool.
- Next, place almond butter and cheese cream in a mixing bowl then using an electric mixer beat until smooth and fluffy.
- Add flax seed mixture to the bowl batter then mix well. Remove the electric mixer.
- After that, stir in toasted almond flour to the batter then using a wooden spatula mix until becoming dough.
- Shape the dough into small balls form then arrange on a baking tray.
- Refrigerate the balls for at least 2 hours or until set.
- Enjoy as dessert whenever you want.

Per Serving: Net Carbs: 2.5g; Calories: 264; Total Fat: 25.4g; Saturated Fat: 13.2g
Protein: 6.6g; Carbs: 3.9g; Fiber: 1.4g; Sugar: 0.5g

Fat 87% / Protein 9% / Carbs 4%

Sweet Date in Savory White Pond

Serves: 4 / Preparation time: 12 minutes / Cooking time: 14 minutes

1-cup coconut flour

1-cup coconut milk

1-tablespoon chopped date

- Preheat a steamer over medium heat then wait until it is ready.
- Prepare 4 aluminum muffin cups then set aside.
- Next, combine coconut flour with coconut milk then stir until smooth and incorporated.
- After that, divide the mixture into 4 prepared aluminum muffin cups then sprinkle chopped date on top.
- Arrange the muffin cups in the steamer and steam for approximately 15 minutes or until set.
- Once it is done, remove from the steamer and arrange on a serving dish.
- Serve and enjoy.

Per Serving: Net Carbs: 3.8g; Calories: 151; Total Fat: 14.6g; Saturated Fat: 12.9g
Protein: 1.7g; Carbs: 5.9g; Fiber: 2.1g; Sugar: 3.5g

Fat 87% / Protein 3% / Carbs 10%

Crispy Broccoli Bites with Cheese

Serves: 4 / Preparation time: 12 minutes / Cooking time: 13 minutes

1 ½ cups broccoli florets

¾ cup almond flour

½ cup grated cheese

2 eggs

½ teaspoon pepper

½ cup extra virgin olive oil, to fry

¼ cup mayonnaise

- Place broccoli florets in a food processor then process until smooth.
- Add almond flour, grated cheese, and eggs to the food processor then season with pepper. Process until becoming dough.
- Take about a tablespoon of dough then shape into small ball form. Repeat with the remaining dough.
- Next, preheat a frying pan over medium heat then pour olive oil into it.
- Once the oil is hot, put the broccoli bites into the frying pan and fry until all sides of the balls are lightly golden brown.
- Remove the broccoli bites from the frying pan and strain the excessive oil.
- Arrange the fried broccoli bites on a serving dish then serve with mayonnaise.
- Enjoy!

Per Serving: Net Carbs: 5.9g; Calories: 404; Total Fat: 39.7g; Saturated Fat: 8.2g
Protein: 8.5g; Carbs: 7.4g; Fiber: 1.5g; Sugar: 2g

Fat 88% / Protein 6% / Carbs 6%

Strawberry Cheesy Pie

Serves: 4 / Preparation time: 12 minutes / Cooking time: 16 minutes

¾ cup almond flour

¼ cup almond butter

1 egg

½ cup fresh strawberries

2 tablespoons goat cheese

½ cup almond yogurt

- Preheat an oven to 350°F (177°C) and coat a pie pan with cooking spray. Set aside.
- Next, place almond butter and egg in a mixing bowl then using an electric mixer beat until just combined. Remove the electric mixer.
- Add almond flour to the mixture then using a wooden spatula mix until becoming dough.
- Place the dough in the prepared pie pan then press on the bottom and sides.
- Once the oven is ready, place the pie in the oven and bake for approximately 10 minutes or until the top of the pie is lightly golden brown. Remove from oven and let it cool.
- Place fresh strawberries in the food processor then process until smooth. Set aside.
- After that, combine the goat cheese with almond yogurt and stir until combined.
- Once the pie is cool, spread strawberries over the pie and top with the goat cheese mixture.
- Store the pie in the refrigerator for at least 2 hours before serving.
- Enjoy cold!

Per Serving: Net Carbs: 6.7g; Calories: 236; Total Fat: 20.7g; Saturated Fat: 3.1g
Protein: 12.1g; Carbs: 11.6g; Fiber: 4.9g; Sugar: 4.1g

Fat 79% / Protein 11% / Carbs 10%

Avocado Chocolate Creamy Pudding

Serves: 4 / Preparation time: 9 minutes / Cooking time: 13 minutes

2 ripe avocados

2-½ tablespoons cocoa powder

½ teaspoon cinnamon

2 tablespoons coconut milk

- Cut the avocados into halves then discard the seeds.
- Scoop out the avocado flesh then place in a food processor.
- Add cocoa powder to the food processor then pour coconut milk into the food processor. Process until smooth.
- Divide the mixture into 4 and put into the serving pots.
- Once it is done, sprinkle cinnamon on top then serve.
- Enjoy!

Per Serving: Net Carbs: 6.7g; Calories: 236; Total Fat: 20.7g; Saturated Fat: 3.1g
Protein: 12.1g; Carbs: 11.6g; Fiber: 4.9g; Sugar: 4.1g

Fat 85% / Protein 10% / Carbs 5%

Coconut Lemon Cake

Serves: 4 / Preparation time: 11 minutes / Cooking time: 19 minutes

1-cup coconut flour

¼ cup almond flour

¼ cup extra virgin olive oil

4 eggs

¼ cup lemon juice

1-teaspoon grated lemon zest

¼ cup coconut flakes

- Preheat an oven to 350°F (177°C) and line a small baking pan with parchment paper. Set aside.
- Place coconut flour, almond flour, and grated lemon zest in a mixing bowl then add the eggs to the bowl.
- Using an electric mixer mix until smooth and fluffy.
- Next, pour lemon juice to the bowl then beat until incorporated.
- Remove the electric mixer then add coconut flakes to the bowl. Using a wooden spatula mix until just combined.
- Transfer the batter to the prepared baking pan and spread evenly.
- Place the baking pan in the oven and bake for approximately 15 minutes or until a toothpick that is inserted to the cake comes out clean.
- Once it is done, remove the cake from the oven and let it cool for a few minutes.
- Take the cake out of the baking pan and cut into slices.
- Arrange the sliced cakes on a serving dish and serve.
- Enjoy.

Per Serving: Net Carbs: 1.9g; Calories: 230; Total Fat: 21.5g; Saturated Fat: 5.5g
Protein: 6.7g; Carbs: 3.9g; Fiber: 2g; Sugar: 1.3g

Fat 84% / Protein 13% / Carbs 3%

Cheesy Pumpkin Balls

Serves: 4 / Preparation time: 12 minutes / Cooking time: 22 minutes

1-cup cream cheese

½ cup pumpkin puree

¾ cup almond butter

1-cup coconut flour

½ teaspoon pumpkin spice

¼ teaspoon ground clove

¼ teaspoon nutmeg

1-tablespoon extra virgin olive oil

- Preheat an oven to 350°F (177°C) and line a baking tray with parchment paper.
- Place cream cheese in a mixing bowl then using an electric mixer beat until soft.
- Add almond butter together with pumpkin spice, ground clove, and nutmeg to the mixing bowl then beat until fluffy.
- Stir in pumpkin puree to the mixture then mix until incorporated. Remove the electric mixer.
- After that, add coconut flour to the mixture then using a wooden spatula mix until becoming dough.
- Shape the dough into small balls then arrange on the prepared baking tray.
- Brush the top of the balls with extra virgin olive oil then bake for approximately 20 minutes or until done and cooked through.
- Once it is done, remove the balls from the oven and place on the cooling rack.
- When the cookies are cool, transfer to a serving dish then serve.
- Enjoy!

Per Serving: Net Carbs: 4.4g; Calories: 278; Total Fat: 26g; Saturated Fat: 13.9g
Protein: 5.9g; Carbs: 6.6g; Fiber: 2.4g; Sugar: 1.5g

Fat 85% / Protein 9% / Carbs 6%

Almond Savory Cookies

Serves: 4 / Preparation time: 19 minutes / Cooking time: 11 minutes

1 cup almond flour

¼ cup almond butter

2 tablespoons extra virgin olive oil

2 eggs

½ cup chopped roasted almonds

- Preheat an oven to 350°F (177°C) and line a small baking tray with parchment paper. Set aside.
- Place almond butter and eggs in a mixing bowl then using an electric mixer beat until smooth and fluffy.
- Pour extra virgin olive oil into the batter then stir well. Remove the electric mixer.
- Add almond flour to the batter then using a wooden spatula mix until combined.
- Take a small scoop of batter then drop on the prepared baking tray. Repeat with the remaining batter.
- Sprinkle chopped roasted almonds on top then bake for approximately 10 minutes or until set and the top of the cookies is lightly golden brown.
- Once it is done, remove the cookies from the oven and transfer to a cooling rack.
- When the cookies are cool, arrange them in a jar with a lid then serve.
- Enjoy.

Per Serving: Net Carbs: 2.1g; Calories: 206; Total Fat: 19.5g; Saturated Fat: 2.5g
Protein: 7g; Carbs: 4.2g; Fiber: 2.1g; Sugar: 0.9g

Fat 85% / Protein 11% / Carbs 4%

Cheesy Pumpkin Puree

Serves: 4 / Preparation time: 4 minutes / Cooking time: 12 minutes

1-cup pumpkin puree

1 cup almond butter

2 tablespoons almond flour

¼ cup coconut milk

2 tablespoons chopped roasted pecans

½ cup grated cheddar cheese

- Preheat an oven to 250°F (121°C) and line a baking tray with parchment paper.
- Spread the almond flour over the baking tray then roast for 5 minutes.
- Remove the almond flour from the oven and let it cool.
- Combine pumpkin puree, almond butter, and almond flour in a bowl then mix well.
- Pour coconut milk over the mixture then stir until incorporated.
- After that, add chopped roasted pecans to the mixture then mix until just combined.
- Divide the mixture into 4 cups then sprinkle grated cheddar cheese on top.
- Refrigerate the dessert for at least an hour before serving then enjoy cold!

Per Serving: Net Carbs: 3.1g; Calories: 140; Total Fat: 11.6g; Saturated Fat: 6.4g
Protein: 5.5g; Carbs: 4.8g; Fiber: 1.7g; Sugar: 1.8g

Fat 75% / Protein 16% / Carbs 9%

Very Berry Nutty Crumbles

Serves: 4 / Preparation time: 12 minutes / Cooking time: 16 minutes

1-tablespoon extra virgin olive oil

1-cup fresh strawberries

½ cup fresh blueberries

¼ cup fresh blackberries

¼ cup fresh raspberries

1 cup chopped almonds

½ cup chopped pecans

2 tablespoons almond butter

1 ½ teaspoon cinnamon

- Preheat an oven to 400°F (204°C) and prepare a casserole dish.
- Preheat a skillet over medium heat then pour olive oil into it.
- Stir in strawberries, blueberries, blackberries, and raspberries then cook until softened.
- Transfer the softened berries to the prepared casserole dish then spread evenly.
- Place chopped almonds and pecans into a food processor then add butter to the food processor. Process until smooth.
- Put the nut mixture into a plastic then pipe over the berries.
- Sprinkle cinnamon on top then place in the oven. Bake for 10 minutes or until crispy on top.
- Once it is done, remove the casserole dish from the oven and let it cool.
- Serve and enjoy.

Per Serving: Net Carbs: 6.9g; Calories: 264; Total Fat: 22.5g; Saturated Fat: 4.8g
Protein: 8.1g; Carbs: 11.4g; Fiber: 4.5g; Sugar: 5.2g

Fat 77% / Protein 13% / Carbs 10%

REFERENCES AND RESOURCES

Belahsen, R., & Rguibi, M. (2006). Population health and Mediterranean diet in southern Mediterranean countries. *Public Health Nutrition, 9*(8A). doi: 10.1017/s1368980007668517

Clarke, C. What is the Ketogenic Diet? A Comprehensive Beginner's Guide. Retrieved from https://www.ruled.me/guide-keto-diet/

Fogelholm, M., Anderssen, S., Gunnarsdottir, I., & Lahti-Koski, M. (2012). Dietary macronutrients and food consumption as determinants of long-term weight change in adult populations: a systematic literature review. *Food & Nutrition Research, 56*(1), 19103. doi: 10.3402/fnr.v56i0.19103

Haber, B. (1997). The Mediterranean diet: a view from history. *The American Journal Of Clinical Nutrition, 66*(4), 1053S-1057S. doi: 10.1093/ajcn/66.4.1053s

Hallböök, T., Lundgren, J., & Rosén, I. (2007). Ketogenic Diet Improves Sleep Quality in Children with Therapy-resistant Epilepsy. *Epilepsia, 48*(1). doi: 10.1111/j.1528-1167.2006.00834.x

Kamb, S. The Beginner's Guide to the Keto Diet: Literally Everything You Need to Know. Retrieved from https://www.nerdfitness.com/blog/the-beginners-guide-to-the-keto-diet-or-ketogenic-diet/

Krikorian, R., Shidler, M., Dangelo, K., Couch, S., Benoit, S., & Clegg, D. (2012). Dietary ketosis enhances memory in mild cognitive impairment. *Neurobiology Of Aging, 33*(2), 425.e19-425.e27. doi: 10.1016/j.neurobiolaging.2010.10.006

Lowery, R., & Wilson, J. (2017). *The Ketogenic Diet: An Authoritative Guide to Ketosis*(1st ed.). Nevada: Victory Belt Publishing.

Martinez-Lacoba, R., Pardo-Garcia, I., Amo-Saus, E., & Escribano-Sotos, F. (2018). Mediterranean diet and health outcomes: a systematic meta-review. *European Journal Of Public Health*. doi: 10.1093/eurpub/cky113

Moore, J., & Westman, E. (2014). *Keto Clarity: Your Definitive Guide to the Benefits of a Low-Carb, High-Fat Diet* (1st ed.). Nevada: Victory Belt Publishing.

Paoli, A. (2014). Ketogenic Diet for Obesity: Friend or Foe?. *International Journal Of Environmental Research And Public Health, 11*(2), 2092-2107. Doi:

10.3390/ijerph110202092

Paoli, A., Rubini, A., Volek, J., & Grimaldi, K. (2013). Beyond weight loss: a review of the therapeutic uses of very-low-carbohydrate (ketogenic) diets. *European Journal Of Clinical Nutrition, 67*(8), 789-796. doi: 10.1038/ejcn.2013.116

Paoli, A., & Bosco, G. (2015). The Ketogenic Mediterranean Diet. *The Mediterranean Diet*, 271-280. doi: 10.1016/b978-0-12-407849-9.00025-7

Paoli, A., Cenci, L., & Grimaldi, K. (2011). Effect of ketogenic mediterranean diet with phytoextracts and low carbohydrates/high-protein meals on weight, cardiovascular risk factors, body composition and diet compliance in Italian council employees. *Nutrition Journal, 10*(1). doi: 10.1186/1475-2891-10-112

Pérez-Guisado, J., Muñoz-Serrano, A., & Alonso-Moraga, Á. (2008). Spanish Ketogenic Mediterranean diet: a healthy cardiovascular diet for weight loss. *Nutrition Journal, 7*(1). doi: 10.1186/1475-2891-7-30

Phinney, S., Bistrian, B., Evans, W., Gervino, E., & Blackburn, G. (1983). The human metabolic response to chronic ketosis without caloric restriction: Preservation of submaximal exercise capability with reduced carbohydrate oxidation. *Metabolism, 32*(8), 769-776. doi: 10.1016/0026-0495(83)90106-3

Romagnolo, D., & Selmin, O. (2017). Mediterranean Diet and Prevention of Chronic Diseases. *Nutrition Today, 52*(5), 208-222. Doi: 10.1097/nt.0000000000000228

Titlow, M. (2017). The Definitive Guide to Micronutrients in the Keto Diet. Retrieved from https://www.compoundsolutions.com/news/micronutrients-in-the-ketogenic-diet

Volek, J., Phinney, S., Kossoff, E., Eberstein, J., & Moore, J. (2011). *The art and science of low carbohydrate living*. Lexington, Ky.: Beyond Obesity.

THE "DIRTY DOZEN" AND "CLEAN 15"

Every year, the Environmental Working Group releases a list of the produce with the most pesticide residue (Dirty Dozen) and a list of the ones with the least **chance of having residue (Clean 15). It's based on analysis from the U.S.** Department of Agriculture Pesticide Data Program report.

The Environmental Working Group found that 70% of the 48 types of produce tested had residues of at least one type of pesticide. In total there were 178 different pesticides and pesticide breakdown products. This residue can stay on veggies and fruit even after they are washed and peeled. All pesticides are toxic to humans and consuming them can cause damage to the nervous system, reproductive system, cancer, a weakened immune system, and more. Women who are pregnant can expose their unborn children to toxins through their diet, and continued exposure to pesticides can affect their development.

This info can help you choose the best fruits and veggies, as well as which ones you should always try to buy organic.

The Dirty Dozen

- Strawberries
- Spinach
- Nectarines
- Apples
- Peaches
- Celery
- Grapes
- Pears
- Cherries
- Tomatoes
- Sweet bell peppers
- Potatoes

The Clean 15

- Sweet corn
- Avocados
- Pineapples
- Cabbage
- Onions
- Frozen sweet peas
- Papayas
- Asparagus
- Mangoes
- Eggplant
- Honeydew
- Kiwi
- Cantaloupe
- Cauliflower
- Grapefruit

MEASUREMENT CONVERSION TABLES

Volume Equivalents (Dry)

US Standard	Metric (Approx.)
¼ teaspoon	1 ml
½ teaspoon	2 ml
1 teaspoon	5 ml
1 tablespoon	15 ml
¼ cup	59 ml
½ cup	118 ml
1 cup	235 ml

Weight Equivalents

US Standard	Metric (Approx.)
½ ounce	15 g
1 ounce	30 g
2 ounces	60 g
4 ounces	115 g
8 ounces	225 g
12 ounces	340 g
16 oz or 1 lb	455 g

Volume Equivalents (Liquid)

US Standard	US Standard (ounces)	Metric (Approx.)
2 tablespoons	1 fl oz	30 ml
¼ cup	2 fl oz	60 ml
½ cup	4 fl oz	120 ml
1 cup	8 fl oz	240 ml
1 ½ cups	12 fl oz	355 ml
2 cups or 1 pint	16 fl oz	475 ml
4 cups or 1 quart	32 fl oz	1 L
1 gallon	128 fl oz	4 L

Oven Temperatures

Fahrenheit (F)	Celsius (C) (Approx)
250°F	120°C
300°F	150°C
325°F	165°C
350°F	180°C
375°F	190°C
400°F	200°C
425°F	220°C
450°F	230°C

INDEX

CPSIA information can be obtained
at www.ICGtesting.com
Printed in the USA
BVHW010236201218
536068BV00013B/1326/P